Queen of the Persians

(the life story of Queen Esther)

Leon Edgar

Copyright © 2015 Leon Edgar

All rights reserved.

ISBN: 1519251793
ISBN-13: 978-1519251794

The sky grew yellow in colour as dawn finally broke over the Zagros Mountains and the herald blew his horn to rouse the troops. Thousands of them woke and began to ready the royal caravan.

'Is it time?' asked the voice in the largest tent.

The older man beside him nodded. 'It is time, my Lord King. By high sun, we should be in Shushan and your people will welcome you and honour you.'

'If only there was a way to avoid it, Haman. I hate such pomp and circumstance.'

'It is necessary, my Lord King. With respect, you are no longer merely King of Babylon. Now that your father has passed into the realm of the gods, you must assume the full responsibility of World Emperor over all the jurisdictional districts belonging to Media and Persia.'

Khshayarsha nodded gravely. 'So be it, my good friend. You have served me well as advisor while I have been co-ruler with my father. Will you remain with me when I am sole King?'

'I would gladly do so, my Lord King, if that is your wish. I am of the Magi and will therefore speak the words of our chief god, Ahura-Mazda. He will guide you in the way to rule your mighty empire.'

'Then you will speak his words to me, Haman. And I will listen and obey.'

The Magi bowed. 'It is the way of the gods, my Lord King.'

Khshayarsha rose to his feet. 'I must bathe before I inspect the Immortals.'

Haman raised the tent flap to call a servant. 'I will arrange water for you, my Lord King.'

'Nonsense. I will bathe in the river. Please see that Artabanus has the troops ready for inspection in one hour.'

'As you command, Sire.' Haman bowed once more and

backed out of the tent as several young women entered to attend to the King.

With entourage in tow, thirty-four-year-old King Khshayarsha of Persia strode towards the waters of the mighty Choaspes as the sun began to feel warm on his face. Dismissing all but a few, he stepped into the ice-cold river and sat on a rock as his assistants began to smooth the water over his strong, manly body. Khshayarsha closed his eyes to the bright spring sun as the cool waters washed away the dust from the road and the sweat of the night.

After twelve years as co-ruler with his father, was he yet ready for the responsibility ahead of him? He would have problems, he knew, from his older brother Artabazanes. Long before his death, their father had decreed that he, Khshayarsha, should rule, but there might well be objections to face. Also, there was his brother-in-law to consider. As General of the land forces, Mardonius wielded much power. If the worst came to the worst, he may have to call on the ten thousand Immortals to defend the throne. Only he himself could rule in the way his father had wished.

The King opened his eyes as the bathing stopped and his attendants started to mutter among themselves. 'What is it?' he asked, a little annoyed at the disturbance.

The eldest maid bowed low. 'With respect, highness, there is a body in the river.'

He instinctively stood up to get out of the impure liquid and stared towards the place where the roaring waters rushed over and between rocks, before gathering themselves to plunge over the edge into the deep Karkhem ravine.

'It is a child,' he said with feeling. 'Send for soldiers. We must recover the body so it may be buried with honour.'

'Very well, Highness,' said the woman who rushed away to

do her ruler's bidding.

'It moved!' shouted one of the other girls excitedly. 'The child lives.'

Khshayarsha instinctively stepped forward and, as he watched, the head moved slightly. Despite calls from his people, the King waded into the water.

Suddenly, the voice of Haman prevailed. 'My Lord King, it is too dangerous. Let one of the men go.'

The King hesitated. His advisor was right. Already, the raging waters were tugging at his legs, threatening to pull him over the lip of the precipice and, between himself and the rock, there was a thrusting torrent which washed away everything in its path. He motioned and three or four young soldiers plunged into the mainstream and worked their way towards the rock. Inch by inch, the men edged closer, holding onto one other to prevent themselves being swept away by the current. When within ten feet of the rock, one slipped and it took all the strength of the others to prevent him plunging to destruction. The King watched as, time after time, they tried and failed until, unexpectedly, a shadow fell over him.

'I go,' said the deep voice and Khshayarsha looked up at the giant beside him.

'It is dangerous, Hegai,' said the King.

The big man pulled back his shoulders and flexed the muscles in his back and bull neck. 'I go,' he insisted and strode forward into the water.

'Take a rope, Hegai,' suggested one of the men. 'We will hold the end and prevent you going over the edge.'

The giant turned and nodded. Within a few minutes, they had knotted a long hemp rope around his waist and he was inching into the raging water. Slowly, he pushed against the current and side-stepped towards the prone figure stretched over the rock as if in sacrifice. Suddenly, he lost his footing and slipped into the water and disappeared under the surface. The men on the bank held on tight to the rope and bore the big man's weight as he vanished over the edge. They slipped and skidded on the muddy limestone bank until several others joined in the tug-of-war with death. Gradually, Hegai was hauled back up and he hung onto the rock to rest.

'You pull now!' he shouted and swung his great body out across the foaming brink. Several times, they tried the manoeuvre until, with a gasp, he clutched hold of the slippery rock and looped the rope over it.

It was a mistake. Under the weight of two, it shifted and, before he could react, the young child was tipped into the frothing torrent. Hegai let go of the rock and grabbed the long hair in passing. He swung the child round and held it with his strong legs as he fought for breath. Slowly, Hegai hoisted the child into the crook of his arm and then looked round at the situation he was in. Whilst holding on to the limp form, he had only one arm free and it had taken both his hands to get to where he now was. He was stuck at the end of a rope while the icy flood waters from the snow melt of the Zagros Mountains cascaded over them both.

The King was quick to observe the predicament of his senior eunuch. 'You men. Move further round and hold the rope tightly. We are going to swing them in to the side.'

Men nodded and moved, others arriving to tie more ropes to the first. The King slithered down the side of the waterfall and raised his arm in signal. The first men let go of their line and the mighty Hegai swung like a pendulum across the main body of water. Gradually, the men hauled and pulled until, with a great cry, Hegai hurled himself onto the cliff path. For one dreadful moment, Khshayarsha was sure he had lost them both. However, he had underestimated the strength of the big man who pulled himself to safety and lay, panting, on the cliff path.

The King was the first on the scene and he gently turned the child over onto her back. 'Why,' he said with feeling. 'It is a young girl and she is beautiful.'

'She may also be badly hurt,' said the Captain of the Guard. 'With your permission, highness, I will have the men take her to Haman.'

The King stood up and nodded. He had seen a great many women and girls in his life and, already, he had gathered a harem of a dozen or more concubines from Babylon in addition to his own queen, Amestris. However, young though she may still be, this child already had the basis for much more beauty than all of them put together. As he watched, the procession made its way back to the camp and the girl was placed in front of the Magi.

'Leave me,' Haman told the soldiers. 'Oil and balsam,' he commanded the servants and, several minutes later, she lay before him as he examined her carefully.

The King raised one eyebrow in a request for diagnosis.

'There would appear to be no bones broken, my Lord King. However, the girl has been badly hurt here,' he pointed to her lower ribs and then her flat belly, 'And here.'

'Can you heal her?'

'I know not how long she has been in the water. I would think most of the night and who knows what damage the cold may have done to her? Additionally, she may be damaged inside. I cannot tell until she wakes and can tell me where the pain is.'

'You can save her life?'

Haman shrugged. 'She is in the hands of Zurvan, the god of

time and destiny. I will do only what I can.'

Khshayarsha smiled. 'The gods are with us, my friend. Have we not saved her from Azhdahak, the dragon of the deep? Mithra will be generous and spare her life so that she may serve me at Shushan the Castle.'

'We have to consider how she came to be in the river, Highness; where she came from.'

'You are right.' He turned to a guard. 'Send Artabanus to me at once.'

The soldier left and, a few moments later, a man of around fifty entered in the uniform of a High General. 'My Lord King?'

'Send scouts to search upstream. The girl's family must be somewhere nearby. They will be missing her.

Artabanus nodded. 'It shall be done.' He left to give the order.

'Well?' said the King to Haman who was now carefully rubbing soothing balsam into the skin of the girl's belly.

'I cannot tell, highness. She is starting a fever.'

'How soon will you know?'

'Not today,' Haman replied. 'I ask your permission to remain here with her while you continue your journey to Shushan.'

'We will all wait.'

'With respect, Highness,' the Magi grovelled. 'You are expected. The Queen will have arranged a great banquet for you.'

The mention of Queen Amestris caused Khshayarsha to stiffen. His marriage had been a political one, arranged by his father in an effort to keep the peace with the Babylonians. He had tried to live up to his responsibilities not only as ruler but also as husband, but Amestris continually flaunted her acquired position, often to the detriment of the Empire. One day, he thought to himself, that woman will go too far.

Khshayarsha looked down at the child with sadness. 'She is so like my own daughter, Haman. Do everything you can for her.'

'I will treat her as if she was one of your own children, my Lord King.'

Khshayarsha smiled and laid his hand on Haman's shoulder. 'I have total confidence in you.'

'My Lord King. May that always be true. I will serve you with honour as I did your father.'

The King watched him working and asked, 'Are there many as loyal as yourself?'

'I regret, not many, Your Highness. There are Carshena, Shethar, Admatha, and Tarshish of the Persians as well as Meres and Marsena of the Medes. They would each serve you unto death.'

'Then they will be my advisors in Shushan.'

'By the law of the Achaemenids, you will need seven.'

'You, my friend, will lead them as my Chief Advisor, my Prime Minister.'

Haman bowed to hide his sly smile of triumph. 'I am honoured, Sire. What of Hegai?'

'Hegai is no longer eunuch of the concubines. I shall give that position to Sha-ashgaz. For his bravery today, Hegai shall become eunuch only to the Queen and her daughters.'

Haman bowed. 'It shall be as you have spoken, my Lord King.'

The King left and Haman and his assistants continued to minister to the girl as she lay on the couch. Outside, the hustle and bustle of an army getting ready to march sounded across the narrow valley.

In the midst of the preparations, several riders drew up and prostrated themselves before Khshayarsha. 'We have found the remains of a wagon on the road from Babylon, my Lord King. It has been recently burned by fire and there are two bodies.'

The King's heart grew sad. 'The child's parents perhaps?'

The Captain nodded. 'I fear so, Sire. The man looked as if he had been struck down with a sword but the woman...'

'Go on, man.'

'She... she had been tied for rape.'

The King's anger flared. 'Who would do such a thing?'

The Captain looked down. 'I can vouch for my men, Sire. Not one of them would do such a thing in peace time.'

'I need to know,' roared the King. He called for the Commander of the Armies. 'Artabanus, investigate this matter fully. I will not rest until the perpetrators of this evil crime are brought to justice.' He turned to Haman. 'Let it this day be written into the law of the Persians and Medes. Whoever did this foul deed shall pay by being dismembered and his house will become a public privy. From now on rape within the city limits or even outside in peacetime is punishable by death.'

'Sire, by Achaemenid tradition, once a law has been written it cannot be changed.'

The King turned on his Chief Advisor. 'You would presume to change my law?'

Haman drew himself erect. 'Never, Highness. You are the Ahasuerus, King of Kings. Your word is the word of Lord Ahura-Mazda.'

The King relaxed. 'I confess I am upset over this matter.'

'My Lord King,' soothed the Magi. 'I feel as you do.'

Khshayarsha glanced down at the prone form in front of him. 'If I had the guilty ones before me now, I would give them to Hegai who, I am sure, would tear them apart with his bare hands.'

THE royal city of Shushan was full of sound. A public holiday had been declared for the arrival of the King from Babylon and everyone was in the streets to welcome him. The already-present Queen, on the other hand, had a headache.

'I do wish those people wouldn't make such a noise,' she sighed. 'Can we not keep them quiet?'

'I fear not, Queen Amestris,' replied her young Maid-of-Honour. 'Your husband the King is due into the city at any moment.'

The older woman glanced at the sun. 'He is late, as usual.'

'Messengers say he was held up at the Choaspes Cataract, Your Majesty.'

'Floods?'

'No, your Majesty. Something about a child being found in the river.'

'A child?' Amestris was furious. 'All this upset because of a mere child?'

'I understand that the child's parents were murdered in the most terrible manner and that the King has sworn vengeance.'

'Has Khshayarsha not got enough to do without involving himself in the petty affairs of the peasants?'

The maid thought it wisest not to answer as her Queen paced the room, wringing her hands. 'It is so hot here. Why did we have to move from Babylon where at least the wind kept us cool? Here in Shushan it is sweltering the whole time.'

'With respect, Your Majesty, this is springtime. In summer, it is considerably hotter.'

Amestris whirled around. 'Hotter? How can we live with it hotter?'

'The Court retires to the old Median capital of Ecbatana in the mountains. It is cooler there.'

'I should hope so. In fact, I ought to be there now.' The

Queen waved her arms. 'And these flies. I hate it here.'

A loud shouting arose from outside and the maid rushed with excitement to the window. 'It is the King.'

'Oh, at last,' sighed the Queen. 'Now, perhaps, we shall get some peace and quiet.'

'But, your Majesty. There is to be a banquet which is decreed to last for seven days. It is the custom.'

'Seven days? And I suppose all they will talk about is wars and armies. There are times when I wish I was not the daughter of the High Priest of Babylon. Perhaps, then, I could just go and hide away from all this fuss over nothing. Khshayarsha has been already been King for twelve years. Why on earth is there all this fuss just because he now rules from Shushan?'

'It is the law of the Achaemenids, your Majesty. There are traditions to be maintained. The laws of the Persians and the Medes are different to those of Babylon.'

'Then perhaps they should be changed,' the Queen retorted angrily. 'They are out of date.'

'They cannot be changed, Your Majesty. Mithra, the son of god, has stated that laws must remain unchanged forever. We do not risk his wrath by even daring to challenge them.'

Amestris lost her temper completely and whirled on her maid. 'Artaynte, you are but a child who is here under sufferance. You would seek to dictate to me? Your Queen?'

'Certainly not,' the teenager said as she bowed low. 'I only answer your questions with truth.'

'Leave me,' the Queen commanded. 'I will call you when I am ready to be dressed.'

'With respect, Your Majesty, the King will expect to be greeted in the Great Hall.'

'Then he will have to be disappointed. If he asks, tell him I am unwell. Tell him anything you like.'

Artaynte bowed again as she backed out of the Court of Women. 'As you command, Queen Amestris.'

KING Khshayarsha was carried into the city at the head of his Immortals to a rousing shout from the people of Shushan. He smiled as garlands of early flowers were thrown into the roadway ahead of him and the procession wound its way through the main gate and towards the palace as the sun shone bright in a clear, blue sky.

'It is an omen,' called the General from the back of his horse. 'Ahura-Mazda is smiling down upon his new son.'

'I pray that you are right, Artabanus. I will need his help to rule this fine kingdom.'

Khshayarsha continued to wave to his people until the procession finally reached the gates of the palace beyond which the common people were refused entry on pain of death. The King stepped from his portable ivory throne. 'Where is the Queen?'

'I regret she is unwell, my Lord King,' replied a teenage girl beside him.

'Unwell?' For a moment, a dark look crossed his face and then he stopped. 'What is your name?'

'I am Princess Artaynte - daughter of your brother, Masistes.'

His anger gradually subsided until he smiled. 'You have grown up very beautiful, my dear Artaynte. You wish to please me?'

The girl blushed and then bowed her head. 'It would be an honour to serve you in any way you desire.'

'Very well. Come to my rooms tonight.'

Artaynte bowed low. 'As you command, my Lord King.'

HAMAN raised himself from bending over the still form before him. He had tried medicine, he had even tried magic but the girl remained sleeping. As a last resort, he had even tried to exorcise the devil inside her but without success.

He pondered. If he failed, the King would be very angry and that was not to happen at any cost. If the King lost his way now, others would step in for their own ends and this great kingdom would collapse in a matter of months. Not only that, he may well lose his own elevated position, and that would most certainly not do at all.

'Oh great Ahura-Mazda,' he called in frustration. 'Hear me now. I entreat you by all the stars of the heavens to save the life of this child. Join with your son, Mithra, and purge the fever from her body. Give me a sign that she will live so that I may comfort my King.'

'Where am I?' came the little voice as if in answer to his prayer.

'It is a sign from god,' he said in a whisper. He bent down to the girl who shrank away from him. 'Relax, child. I will not harm you. I am Haman of the Magi.'

'Where am I?' she repeated.

'You are in the camp of the great Persian King, Khshayarsha.'

She looked around frantically. 'Where is the giant?'

'Giant?' He paused and then smiled and held up his hand. 'Wait!'

Haman disappeared and the girl looked around at the beautiful furnishings of the tent. Wrapping the blanket around herself, she slipped her feet to the floor and walked round the tent, touching the furs and skins hanging from its roof. A movement made her turn.

'You well?' asked Hegai, standing in the doorway of the tent.

She smiled and nodded. 'I saw you in the river. You saved my life.'

Hegai shrugged. 'Is nothing. You wish eat?'

Hadasseh nodded and the giant held out his hand to her which she took without hesitation.

The sun was low in the sky as they stepped out of the tent together and she looked around at the remnants of the overnight camp. There were several dozen tents and a battalion of soldiers left to guard them. The soldiers shifted to make room for them both at the campfire as they sat and began to eat from a basket of fruit and bread which had been prepared. They watched as the girl tucked in to the food as if she hadn't eaten for a week. Suddenly, she noticed that they were all watching her closely and grew afraid, shuffling close to Hegai for protection. The men laughed.

'You not be afraid, little one,' laughed Hegai. 'They not see child eat so much before.'

She looked wary for a moment until the men started to continue their conversations.

'They the Immortals,' Hegai continued. 'Best of King's troops. When they are in battle, they a sight to see as they advance over hill and valley and nothing stop them.'

'Why are they here?'

'They escort new King from his place of coronation at Pasargadae to Shushan where he to rule as King. Tell me, why you here?'

She looked down. 'My father was to serve the King at Shushan.'

'You know people at city?'

She nodded. 'My father's brother, Jair, was taken there along with the Holy Prophet, Daniel. His son, Mordecai, is there now.'

'Mordecai?' Hegai turned to the guards. 'You men hear of man, Mordecai, in city?'

The soldiers looked at each other and then shook their heads. Suddenly, one had inspiration. 'There is a gatekeeper of the palace called Marduka. Could that be him?'

Hegai looked at the girl who shrugged. 'I have never met my cousin. My father was to make all the arrangements.'

Hegai slipped his arm around her shoulders. 'Who was it who hurt parents?'

She shuddered and shook her head, tears appearing in her eyes. 'I don't know. It was very dark.'

'You recognise again?'

'Possibly. I don't know.'

'You remember names?'

'No. They did say names but they were all strange to me.' Her eyes lit up. 'One was called Arisai, or something like it.'

'Arisai? I know an Arimi, could that be it?'

She shook her head. 'I don't think so. It was all strange and I was very frightened. Father made me hide in the water barrel until I could get away. Then I... I fell over the cliff into the river.'

'I sorry. Not want to remind of death.'

The girl placed her small hand upon that of the giant. 'What is your name?'

He proudly thumped his chest with his fist. 'I, Hegai of Parthia.'

'My name is Hadasseh. From Babylon.'

'Our King and Queen from Babylon.'

'So my father said. I never met him there but father said he saw him once or twice. Mother said he was very good looking.'

Hegai smiled. 'Maybe so. Me not notice.'

'Will you help me find my cousin?'

'We all help. You lonely girl now.'

Hadasseh looked down at her hands in her lap and a tear slowly trickled down her face.

THE Chief Steward was admitted to the royal chambers at Shushan where he bowed before the King.

The King looked up. 'You have news, Harbona?'

The newcomer bowed again. 'I regret it is not good news, my Lord King.'

Khshayarsha faced him. 'Well, don't just stand there. Tell me.'

Harbona looked down at the polished mosaic floor. 'The child has disappeared.'

'Disappeared?' The King started to pace the floor. 'And who was responsible for this... this treachery?'

'Haman and the others arrived in the city the day before yesterday and she was placed in the care of Hegai.'

'I am most surprised at Hegai.'

'It was not entirely his fault, sire. Hegai was summoned by the Queen during the afternoon and he was forced to leave the girl in the charge of some of the other concubines. Unfortunately, the Queen kept Hegai until after dark and, when he returned to the harem, the girl had gone.'

'Did she run away?'

'No-one knows, Your Majesty. They didn't see her leave and the gatekeepers say no stranger passed them.'

'Then she is still somewhere in the palace?'

'If not the palace, then certainly the city.'

'The city is a big place, Harbona. A young child could get lost forever.'

'Your slaves are searching for her, even as we speak.'

The King slammed his fist on the table. 'Why can we not get anything right these days? My father would have had you all executed.'

Harbona bowed before his king. 'I offer you my own life, Your Majesty.'

The King's rage subsided. 'You are a faithful servant, Harbona. Send in the gatekeepers to me. I want a full report of the incident. And,' he added. 'I want that girl found.'

Artaynte strolled over and laid her head on the King's arm. 'I may be able to help.'

'You?'

'I have friends in the market. I could ask them to look out for the girl if she is important to you.'

'She is now an orphan in a strange city. She needs someone to look after her.'

Artaynte's lips curled a little as she slipped her arms around the King's neck. 'Is that all you want of her?'

Khshayarsha drew back a little. 'She can be no more than twelve years old.'

'But you have loved me several times these last few nights and I am little older.'

'That is different. You are of the Queen's household and I am not looking for another concubine. If I ever find this girl, she will become my Queen.'

Artaynte grinned wickedly. 'Amestris would not like that, my Lord King.'

The King grunted. 'Amestris will not be Queen for much longer if she does not please me a little more than she has of late.'

'I hear that she has summoned my mother to Court for the New-Year celebrations.'

'Has she now?' said the King thoughtfully. 'Now why would

she do that?'

'With respect, my Lord King, I believe the Queen thinks you are in love with her.'

Khshayarsha smiled. 'I met her but once, my child, when I visited your father at Sardes. I admit that I was impressed. Like yourself, she is extremely attractive.'

'She is younger than my father, sire. I was born when she was but fifteen. She is only twenty-eight now.'

'That makes her two years younger than Amestris. Mind you, the Queen is now beginning to show her age.'

The girl sat up. 'But Amestris is lovely, your Majesty. Do the people of Babylon not call her Vashti, the Beautiful One?'

'They do, my child. I just wish that she was as beautiful at heart. I suspect that she has an ulterior motive in summoning your mother to Shushan at this time.'

'Surely not. Perhaps she wishes to bestow a great honour on her.'

'It is certainly possible. By tradition, whatever the Queen asks for on New-Year's Day must be granted. If she asks that your mother be honoured in some way, I cannot refuse.'

'Would you anyway? Refuse, that is?'

'Certainly not. My brother has served me well as Satrap of Bythinia. They both deserve great honour and so, my dear, do you.'

'I deserve nothing. I am but your humble servant.'

The King rolled over, grasped the Royal robes and draped them around Artaynte's shoulders. 'They suit you, my dear.'

'But the child...'

'Find this girl from the river for me and you will certainly become her first Maid of Honour.'

Artaynte moved closer to the King and smirked. 'As my name is Artaynte, the child is as good as found.'

QUEEN Amestris checked the arrangements for the New-Year celebrations. The wine jars were filled, the banquet ready. Within the hour, the guests would start to arrive from far and wide and she would be very happy. The slaves straightened the furnishings for the hundredth time until, as last, she was satisfied. Soon, a thousand satraps and governors would be reclining around the room, enjoying the entertainment she had prepared.

She approached the Commander of the Guard. 'You know what to do, Artabanus?'

'Of course, Your Majesty. It shall be just as you have spoken.'

'Very well. Do not fail me tonight.'

'I won't,' he sneered. 'The pleasure will also be mine.'

'I am sure it will,' she smiled. 'I am sure it will.'

KHSHAYARSHA sat with his queen as the guests ate and drank. Dancers pranced around the floor and entertained the men who were steadily getting the worse for drink. The highlight came in the evening as the New Year officially began.

'Your Majesty,' said the Queen as she lounged beside him. 'I ask of you a favour.'

'As is your right, my Queen. Ask it and, up to half my kingdom, I would grant your wish.'

She smiled. 'I want Phratagune.'

'Phratagune? The wife of my brother Masistes?'

'I wish her to be remembered forever in Persia for what she has done.'

He smiled. 'Then she is in your hands, my dear.'

The Queen's eyes went dark. 'Thank you, my Lord King.'

She turned to the Commander of the Guard. 'Artabanus, bring Phratagune to me and do with her just as I have instructed.'

Artabanus bowed lower than he had ever done for the King. 'At you command, Queen Amestris.'

The crowd hushed as the woman in question stood up, still somewhat puzzled, and was escorted to the centre of the room.

Her daughter, Artaynte, watched from the doorway, unable to attend due to her age. Pride filled her young chest as she watched her mother stand before the King and Queen. The royal guard approached and stood formally each side of her. Suddenly, her heart started to beat frantically as Artabanus approached her mother carrying a long javelin and then the young girl shuddered at what she saw and ran screaming from the palace.

KHSHAYARSHA was sad. Despite promises and much searching on the part of the King's servants, Hadasseh was not found and now, on top of that, his niece and favourite concubine, the lovely Artaynte, had also been banished. Over the next few months, he went deeper into depression and the Queen became totally isolated from him. For purposes of prestige, they put on a show but the gap between them grew steadily wider as Khshayarsha found compensation in the arms of his other concubines.

In the spring of the next year, the Court left the city to spend the heat of the summer in the Median capital, Ecbatana, and the city of Shushan was relatively quiet at mid-summer. All the important officials were elsewhere and just the ordinary people were left, protected by Artabanus and his palace guard. In the poor section of the city, a teenager wandered around aimlessly, close to the palace which had been her home for such a short time. She raised the loose gown from her shoulders due to the oppressive heat and then sat down on the stone steps to allow the slight breeze through the gateway to waft over her parched body.

The soldiers manning the gate watched her and, after some time, two of them approached. 'You would please us at off-duty time?'

Artaynte shook her head and protectively wrapped her arms around herself. She may be ex-maid of the Queen, and ex-concubine to the King, but harlot she most definitely was not. However, the men refused to take "no" for an answer and one sat down beside her and reached out his hand to touch her. Artaynte squirmed away from him and attempted to stand but was pulled down viciously. Two of the men held her down as the third started to pull at her clothing until, suddenly, everything went quiet. The young girl looked around in perplexity as the grip on her arm relaxed.

'What are you doing?' asked the middle-aged man in the long, blue gown.

One of the soldiers shrugged. 'Just having some fun, my Lord. It was nothing.'

'Then get back to your posts or I will have you flogged. Do you understand?'

The men hurried about their duties as the girl was left facing the officer from the gatehouse.

'Thank you, my Lord,' she said when she was alone with the newcomer.

The man smiled. 'You look hot, my dear. Would you like a drink?'

Artaynte looked wary for a moment and wondered if she could trust this man, but when he turned and entered his office beside the gate, she followed, slowly and carefully. The interior was dark and it was several moments before her eyes could become accustomed after the harsh glare from outside. The outer office was well-furnished and clean and the man poured fresh water from a jug as she watched and then placed it upon the table in the middle of the room. When the man sat down and pointed to the embossed clay cup, she recognised that he meant her no harm and so shuffled inside and sat down on the wooden bench.

He smiled pleasantly. 'What is your name, child?'

'I...I am Artaynte, my Lord.'

He frowned. 'Princess Artaynte? Daughter of the King's brother?'

'Yes, my Lord.'

'I was sorry to hear about the execution of your family,' he said as she drank thirstily. 'So now you are alone and lost.'

'Yes, my Lord.'

The man smiled again. 'I am not your lord. I am merely Chief of the Gatehouse. You must call me Marduka.'

Artaynte started at the name. 'You are Marduka?' Her heart beat faster. Where had she heard that name before? She could not remember but, somehow, she knew it was important that she should. 'Do you live here alone?' she asked carefully, striving for a clue.

'Only myself and my daughter. She should be home from the market soon and you can meet her.'

'Daughter?'

'Yes,' said the man, still smiling. 'If you can stay awhile, Astur would be glad to have a friend to talk with.'

'Is your daughter young?' she asked, seeing that the man was not as old as her own father had been.

'Astur is but fourteen, my child. About your own age.'

'Oh,' she said and relaxed. Perhaps, after months of being shunned by all but frustrated soldiers, she would find someone to spend time with at last. A shadow fell across the threshold.

'Ah, Astur,' spoke Marduka, rising. 'Come. We have a guest.'

The girl he had called Astur stepped closer with a spring in her step. Artaynte gaped. She had never seen anyone so beautiful in all her life. The girl's long, black hair cascaded about shoulders which were deeply tanned, and her slim body was perched atop long, brown legs. She had a smile which was warm and friendly, one that strayed to her big, brown eyes. Artaynte's heart began to beat faster with excitement. This was no Persian maid and she was definitely not of Shushan. She held her breath momentarily. Could this be...?

'Where do you live?' asked the voice which sounded like music.

'I..I no longer have a home,' replied Artaynte sadly. 'I used to live in the palace but do so no longer.'

'Would you like to stay with us for a while?' asked Astur with a genuine offer of friendship.

'I would like it very much, if that were possible.'

Astur turned to Marduka who smiled and nodded. She held out her hand to Artaynte. 'Come, I will show you my room.'

Hand-in-hand, the two girls climbed the narrow spiral staircase up the inside of one of the gate turrets. There were several small rooms off to the sides and in all her year or so spent in Shushan, Artaynte had no idea such places existed. At the top, the staircase opened out into a big room with a narrow, slit window overlooking the gateway, another which gave a view across the valley to the Zagros, and a third, bigger one, that gave a panorama right across the roofs of the houses. In the background, the walls of the winter palace stood proud and strong.

Artaynte held her breath. 'Why, it is amazing. I can see the whole city.'

'This is my own room,' said Astur kindly. 'You must stay here with me.'

'Do you live here all the time?'

Astur nodded. 'I sleep here while Marduka rests below so as to be available to call the guard quickly if anyone calls unexpectedly.'

Artaynte stiffened with excitement. 'You do not call him "father" but "Marduka". Why is that?'

Astur laughed pleasantly. 'Marduka is not my real father but my cousin. As a kind of foster-father, he has cared for me almost these last two years, since my own parents died.'

Artaynte's heart beat frantically as she stepped closer to the girl and gently placed her hand on her arm.

'You are Hadasseh,' she whispered.

A look of stark terror passed across Hadassah's face and Artaynte was certain. She reached out her hands and gently touched the younger girl's face. 'Don't worry. Marduka helped me outside. I will not betray you.'

Hadasseh sat down. 'How...how did you know?'

'Your name. It means myrtle in both Aramaic and in Aryan.'

'Please don't tell,' said Astur quietly. 'Marduka took me from the palace last year and hid me here.'

'You are my friend,' assured Artaynte. 'I will tell no-one without your permission. After all, we are both in hiding, aren't we?'

Hadasseh relaxed a little and held Artaynte's hands in her own. 'You must teach me these languages you know. Marduka gives me lessons in local customs and the art of writing but I know little of languages except Hebrew and Chaldean.'

'I am a poor maid, Hadasseh. I know only eleven languages.'

'Eleven?'

'My father was the brother of the King and I was maid to the Queen for a while. Languages are easy to learn when you must speak them every day to foreign visitors.'

Hadasseh seemed excited. 'What do you know of the King?'

Artaynte paused. How much should she tell this girl? She decided upon total honesty. If she was to fulfil the plan brewing in her mind, she would need the total trust of this girl.

'I was concubine to the King,' she admitted quietly.

Hadasseh gaped for a moment. 'Is..is the King really kind like they say he is?'

Artaynte smiled. 'He can be. However, when he is angry, everyone is afraid.'

'How did you come to leave the Court?'

Artaynte shrugged. 'The Queen executed the rest of my family.'

'Amestris? She killed your mother and father?'

Artaynte nodded. 'And my brother and sisters. My father was caught whilst trying to escape and was hung. She...she had my sisters disembowelled alive.'

'Ugh! And your mother?'

'She was ritually desecrated at Court.'

'But why?'

'The Queen suspected she was having an affair with the King.'

'And was she?'

The Princess was quick to reply. 'Of course not. My mother was a good woman and the King respected that.' She sighed. 'No, it was me the King was loving. I became one of the royal concubines and, in time, I was to have become wife to Crown

Prince Darius. But that is not possible now.'

'You poor girl.'

Artaynte bowed her head. 'Amestris really hated my mother. She had told the King that she would make sure my mother would be remembered forever. She certainly achieved that.' She looked straight at Hadasseh. 'If I am ever caught by the Queen, I will suffer the same fate.'

AFTER six months of war conference at Ecbatana to discuss the invasion of Greece, Khshayarsha was ready for a banquet. All the Princes of the twenty satrapies of Persia came along with their wives and concubines and, in the city of Shushan, there was hardly a room not taken for the many visitors and guests. It was a busy time for Marduka. Each of the visitors had to be screened against the possibility of assassins entering the city and the guard was doubled in anticipation.

'Will you be all right this evening?' he asked as Hadasseh carefully placed the official headdress of the Royal Gatekeeper upon his head.

'Of course we will,' she laughed in reply. 'I promise we will not leave the gatehouse until you return. We can see the palace from the roof and will watch the festivities from there.'

'You are upset about not coming, aren't you?'

'Not at all, my father. You go and have a good time.' She kissed his cheek. 'Bring me back some fruit of Ethiopia.'

'And some wine,' added Artaynte.

'Wine?' frowned Marduka. 'You are too young to be drinking wine.'

'I am sixteen and Hadasseh is fifteen tomorrow. We are ready for the nectar of the gods.'

Marduka shook his head. These girls were certainly growing

up fast. In another year or less, he could be losing his Astur. When that happened, he knew he would be very sad.

'And lock the door,' he said as he departed.

'Yes, father,' they said in unison and giggled.

THE King paced before his chief advisors who sat around the polished cedar table from the mountains of Lebanon.

'What say you, my brothers? Am I being harsh by insisting upon the presence of the Queen at my banquet?'

'Not at all,' spoke up the Prince of Media. 'Every Queen must do the bidding of her King, regardless of who she is.'

'I agree,' said Admatha. 'Though what my own queen will say now she has seen the example of Amestris, I hate to think.'

'Then I am right?'

'Your Majesty,' said Haman. 'I have served you here at Shushan and your father, Darius, before you. The implications of this matter are indeed very great. Once, the Queen's attitude and actions could simply be described as unusual or unorthodox. But now, things are different. Throughout the Empire, people are saying that their ruler is not a King but the puppet of Queen Amestris of Babylon.'

'And what say you, my friend?'

'I know you well, my Lord King,' Haman said tactfully. 'You have permitted your Queen to act in the way she has so that she will reveal her true motives. Now that she has refused to come to the banquet at your bidding, Ahura-Mazda has given you the opportunity you need to rid the Empire of her once and for all.'

'It seems such a small thing compared to some of her earlier atrocities.'

'Not so. Prince Admatha make a valid point when he says

that her rebellion is a symbol and could have an effect on the households of not just Shushan but of the whole of the Persian Empire. If this is overlooked, from India to Ethiopia, wives will think it right to disobey their masters in the same way.'

'Then what do you propose I do?'

'You must write a law, an unchangeable law according to the law of the Persians and Medes, that whenever a master commands his household, they must obey without question.'

Khshayarsha looked around the group of seven princes. 'Can I do that?'

'You are King,' said Carshena. 'May I also add that if you do not act in this way, it is not just wives who will rebel. Whole nations will see that the King's word amounts to nothing and will challenge your power. The results could be disastrous for this great kingdom we have forged.'

'What say you, Haman?'

'My Lord King, the words which have been spoken are good. If you give the word, let a royal decree go to the length and breadth of the earth, that Queen Amestris be banished from the palace and that all other unruly wives are to be treated in a similar manner.'

The King smiled. 'That does seem good to me.'

'Furthermore,' the Magi added. 'Let a proclamation go forth that you will take a new Queen from among the nations.'

'But it will mean war with Babylon. Shamash-Eriba will not stand for the banishment of his daughter in favour of another queen.'

'I suggest that when he gets back from crushing the Lybians,' said Haman. 'You send Prince Megabyzus to Babylon. If there is trouble, he will deal with it in the most... appropriate manner.'

'You would recommend deliberately provoking a war with

Babylon?'

'Sire. I believe there is a time for leniency and a time for firmness. Deal with Amestris now, while you have the chance and, if they rebel in Babylon, crush them.'

The King looked around his advisors who were agreed. He smiled. 'So let it be written.'

THE war conference over, King Khshayarsha of the Persians signed the last of the documents and Harbona left to see them translated and issued. He turned to another matter.

'Am I doing the right thing, Haman?'

'In arranging war with the Greeks? The gods have decreed it, so it must be right.'

'It will seem like petty revenge to the Ionians. They will think we are simply attacking to avenge the defeat of my father's forces at Marathon.'

'Mardonius has written from Thrace to say that a good push southward now will drive the Macedonians into the sea forever. We may never get another opportunity like this.'

'But what a waste if we lose.'

'We cannot lose, my Lord King. The Greeks are a pathetic lot, divided into a multitude of individual city states and they cannot even agree on boundaries between each other. Athens is at loggerheads with Macedonia, Sparta with Ionia. Strike now and you will conquer them all.'

'I fear you are right, my good friend.' The King stood up and walked to the window.

'You seem distracted, my Lord King.'

'I am still thinking of the complications surrounding the banishment of Queen Amestris.'

'Have the Babylonians declared war?'

The King nodded. 'The news arrived yesterday. Perhaps I should give Shamash-Eriba one last chance to surrender.'

'I say strike now, My Lord King. The princes have agreed to support you with both arms and men.'

'Very well,' he sighed. 'When you leave, send in Megabyzus to me.'

'Before I go, sire, there is one other matter requiring your decision.'

'Yes?'

'The matter of your replacement queen.'

The King sighed. 'I told the other princes how I feel. There can be no other queen until I have found the girl from the river.'

'The men have searched thoroughly for almost three years now and have totally scoured the city, my Lord King. Reluctant though I am to say so, I fear that she has been disposed of by your enemies. If not, she would surely have been found by now.'

'You think the girl is dead?'

The wise man looked down and smiled to himself. 'I fear so, your Majesty.'

'Who would do such a thing?'

'The men who killed her parents, perhaps. If they knew she had lived, they would want to eliminate her lest she identify them. You, yourself, decreed their execution. They will have made very sure they tied up all the loose ends.'

'In some ways, I feel you may be right. On the other hand, I see her in my dreams every night. Somehow, I cannot let go of her memory. While Queen Amestris was in my Court, I forced myself to forget her. Now...I cannot. Somehow, I know she is alive.'

'If she is, then she has not been found because she does not want to be found.'

The King sighed. 'What other alternatives do I have?'

'You could marry one of the many Princesses in the empire. I hear that Princess Juliana of Thrace is very beautiful and such a union would ensure a strong ally on our western front.'

The King stood up and faced the window. 'I will not have another political marriage alliance. Look what has happened because I married the daughter of the High Priest of Marduk. As long as Amestris had her own way, which she always had at home with her father, she was happy. No, enough of political marriages. I want someone whom I can love and trust, someone who will obey me instantly and without question.'

The shrewd Magi then put his plan into operation. 'Then the answer is to select a wife from your concubines. While you are away in Greece, have your harem extended a little to include all the best virgins in the realm and then closely evaluate them upon your return. It will serve two purposes. Firstly, you will have a fine selection from which to choose and, secondly, you will have a vastly improved harem.'

The King smiled. 'You are always so very wise and practical, Haman.'

The Magi smiled at the possibility of his own daughter being chosen as Queen. 'It is how your father would have done it, my Lord King.'

Khshayarsha drew himself erect. 'Then it is how I shall do it. Will you supervise the harem selection?'

The Magi shook his head. No, that would be far too obvious. He smiled. 'I am too old to recognise beauty, My Lord King. I would suggest you leave the whole matter to Hegai. He has your best interests at heart and will not fail you. Have him personally select the maidens for the Harem. You can then spend a little time with each concubine, as is your right as

King, and then choose the best one from among them. There is no rush and even the choosing could be a source of great pleasure in itself.'

'Haman, while you live there will be no-one superior in my kingdom. I speak as King and so let it be written.'

The wise man bowed low as he mentally calculated the value of the bribes which would be necessary. 'It is a great honour, your Majesty.'

'Then serve me just one more time as Chief Advisor before taking up the robes of Prime Minister. Instruct Hegai as you have spoken. Let him evaluate the maidens of the kingdom and select the best. When I return from subduing the Greeks, then I will decide whom from among them is to become Queen of the Persians.'

THE small group of men sat in the semi-darkness plotting a deed which could change the entire make-up of the Persian Empire.

'Do we act now?' asked the tall one.

'No. We must be patient. If we kill the King now, the wrath of the Princes will be directed against us. They will know who has carried out the act.'

'My son is right,' said a third. 'We must be more cautious.'

'Perhaps he could die in battle.'

'That is indeed possible. However, there are also the King's sons to consider. They must die, too.'

'There will be uproar if young Darius and Artakhshayarsha are assassinated.'

'Unless we can arrange it so that they fight amongst themselves.'

'They are yet too young for that. Artakhshayarsha, I know, is jealous of his older brother but he is yet only fourteen. I regret we may have to await the King's return.'

'You may be right.' He paused. 'But what of the new Queen? The King has issued instructions to Hegai to select suitable girls for the Harem. Upon his return, he will choose a queen from among them.'

'May I make a suggestion,' said the older one.

'Of course.'

'Have patience until the selection has been made. When the wedding takes place, we can kill two birds with one stone. Murder the King in his bed and who will be blamed but the new Queen?'

'You are wise, my friend. Then we execute the new Queen as the culprit and deal with the King's sons another time.'

'The people will be angry over the death of their King. He has been lenient with them.'

'Then we will make the new Queen's execution public.'

The tall one sniggered. 'I think Amestris had the right idea with Phratagune. Prolonged abuse and torture followed by public disembowelment.'

The younger one shuddered at the thought. 'That sounds painful.'

'That is the whole point. Her constant screams will be heard throughout the city for many hours and will appease the crowds. I will personally supervise the matter to ensure that she does not die too quickly.'

THE hot, summer sun beat down on the city of Shushan and people went slowly about their daily routine. Few were seen out in the middle of the day as the ground itself seemed to reflect the intense heat up at them. Life in the gatehouse was normal for the time of year as Marduka continued to ensure that the gates to the palace were well guarded while Hadasseh and Artaynte kept house in their stone tower. Fruit became scarce as the heat increased and even the Ulai watercourse which supplied the city with fresh water began to dwindle.

'I must go to the market,' said Hadasseh, rising from her bunk, her smooth skin glistening even in the relative coolness of the gatehouse.

'Very well,' agreed her friend without opening her eyes. 'The heat will lessen as evening approaches. Perhaps, today, there will be word of the King.'

Hadasseh wiped herself with a woollen cloth before slipping her thin shift over her head and heading for the stone steps.

'Be careful,' warned Artaynte.

Hadasseh smiled. 'The city is quiet at this time of day. What harm could befall me?'

The young Princess opened her eyes. 'You are getting too brave with your strolling around the city. You could be recognised. Wear your veil.'

Hadasseh sighed and reached for a head covering. 'You are right.' She smiled. 'I will not be long.'

Skipping down the stairs, she passed her cousin with a kiss and burst out into the bright, parched city. Even through her leather sandals, the road felt hot and, already, her shift was becoming soaked with her perspiration as she lifted it slightly to allow air to pass around her body. Artaynte opened her eyes and slipped quickly off the bed and threw her cloak around her shoulders, fastening the catches as she skittered down the stairs.

'I am just going to the market,' she called to Mordecai as she passed him and he stroked his beard thoughtfully as he watched her disappear quickly up the road.

There was little left at the busy market as Hadasseh reached to touch the few hardened melons left on a stall. With practiced care, she selected the best one for their evening meal and paid out of a small leather purse tied around her wrist.

'Will you have any more by the end of the week?' she queried, dropping her veil so the merchant she always dealt with could hear her words clearly.

'I know not, my Lady. If I have, I will save you the best.'

Hadasseh smiled and her white teeth glistened. 'I would be very grateful.'

The man nodded as the young girl grinned and waved her thanks. As she stepped forward, she abruptly stopped and quickly refastened her veil. The two men across the road were very familiar and an ice-cold wave of panic passed over her. Turning quickly, she found herself running down a side passage and then into a gateway, her heart beating frantically. She was just beginning to breathe again when hands reached out and pulled her down the narrow stairway into a cold cellar. She tried to struggle but a hand was placed firmly over her face as the weight of her assailant's body held her to the stone floor. After several minutes, the two bodies relaxed.

'Do not call out,' whispered her attacker who was still a dark shape against the narrow doorway. 'If I let go will you promise not to cry out?'

As far as she was able, Hadasseh nodded her head and, suddenly, she was free and the other form peered out of the doorway for a moment before returning and kneeling before her.

'You must be more careful,' said the voice. 'You were nearly caught just then.'

'I do not understand.'

'There were people watching you. I knew this might happen

so I followed you.'

'It is not necessary, Artaynte. I am old enough to look after myself.'

'Then why did you panic and run just then.'

'I saw a couple of men I thought I recognised. They were near the house of Haman.'

The Princess leant closer. 'They were the ones who killed your parents?'

'I think so, but I'm not sure.'

'Describe them.'

'Dark hair, beards, long gowns.'

Artaynte smiled. 'You have just described most of the male population of Persia.'

'It is not funny.'

'Did I say it was?'

EVEN in Ecbatana, it was oppressively hot. The mountain streams trickled lazily along parched beds and even the wind which normally blew gently off the high slopes was still.

'Are we ready?' asked Khshayarsha.

'We await only your command, my Lord King,' replied Haman.

'Good. What is the strength of the assembled army?'

'Mardonius awaits you at Sardes, your Majesty. He has collected together five-hundred-thousand footmen and sixty-thousand horsemen from Bythinia and Syria. He has also assembled three-thousand transport ships to keep us supplied and the Phoenicians have provided over a thousand triremes in case there is a sea battle.'

'What about Artabazanes?'

'Your brother awaits you at the Hellespont, my Lord King.

He has persuaded a Greek engineer to construct a bridge of pontoons right across the waterway.'

'That is some feat,' said the Commander of the Guard.

'One you will not see, Artabanus. I need you to remain here to protect Ecbatana and Shushan from attack.' He turned to the General at his elbow. 'Megabyzus, I need you to go to Babylon immediately. I have given Shamash-Eriba enough time to reconsider his foolish action.'

The younger man nodded. 'Do I make peace with him?'

'Not this time. It is time to set an example to the Greeks. Occupy Babylon and execute their High Priest. Do this deed and my own daughter will become yours.'

Megabyzus smiled broadly. 'It shall be done just as you have spoken.'

'Good. When the message of what you have done gets across to Macedonia, perhaps the Greeks will reconsider their rebellion.'

Haman coughed. 'When do we leave, your Majesty?'

'We march with the Immortals and the rest of the Persian army to Sardes in the autumn and we shall winter there.'

'With respect, Sire,' said the Magi. 'Are you still getting the same dream?'

'I am, Haman. Our chief god has made it clear to me that he will no longer tolerate the rebellion in Greece.'

Artabanus interrupted. 'My Lords, I too have had this dream.'

'It is the will of Ahura-Mazda,' confirmed Haman.

'So, to review,' said the King. 'Artabanus stays in Persia, Megabyzus goes to Babylon and enforces the peace, we meet Mardonius at Sardes and then Artabazanes at Thrace. Tygranes will lead the Immortals and we will crush these pagans for ever.'

'Would I come with you?' asked Haman.

'How would I manage without my Magi to cast lots? You and I must go otherwise Mardonius and Artabazanes will end up fighting each other instead of the Greeks.'

Everyone laughed but, in their hearts, each of them knew that the King had just spoken words of pure truth.

AUTUMN turned to winter and another year began. Khshayarsha and his army marched north-west along the Royal Highway, collecting battalion after battalion of extra men as they went. Through Phrygia and Cappadocia they marched until, with a force of over two million armed men, they wintered at Sardes. By Spring, the pontoon bridge across the Hellespont was complete and, as the first of the spring flowers pushed their heads through the dark soil of Anatolia, the immense Persian war machine converged on Macedonia.

ALREADY, people were leaving Shushan for the mountains. It was yet Springtime but the palace was almost empty and the heat once again oppressive.

'The city is quiet, my father,' said Astur as they ate a midday meal.

'Almost everyone has left, Hadasseh. There are just the Harem supervisors in the palace.'

'That is odd,' frowned Artaynte. 'Why have they stayed behind?'

'To supervise the choosing of the Royal Harem in readiness for the King's return. Khshayarsha has given the command that his harem of concubines be extended so that, upon his return, he can choose a new queen from among them.'

'Are you hoping to become one of the royal concubines again, Artaynte, now that Amestris has gone for good?'

'Alas, Hadasseh, such a thing is not possible. The immediate danger from Amestris has gone, I know, but there was my promise to the King to find you. Until I can live up to my sworn oath, by the law of the King I must remain banished from his presence.'

'What if you could fulfil your promise?' asked Mordecai quietly.

Hadasseh turned to face him. 'Do you realise what you are saying, my father?'

Mordecai nodded. 'Yes, I think so.'

'You are suggesting I consent to becoming a royal concubine, a mere toy for the King's pleasure?'

'It will not be like that, Hadasseh my child. The position of concubine is a great privilege, second only to the Queen and the Royal Princes.'

Hadasseh stood up. 'I cannot do it. You do not know what you are asking of me.'

Artaynte placed her hand over her friend's. 'What troubles you, Hadasseh?'

'After what happened to my mother on the road from Babylon, I will let no man ever use me that way.'

'It does not need to be like that,' soothed Artaynte. 'I was with the King for many nights and his love was like the balsam of Gilead. He is kind and loving, not at all like the men who raped and killed your mother.'

'I will not do it,' Hadasseh insisted. 'I feel sick at the very thought of anyone touching me.'

'There will be no pain,' reasoned the Princess. 'I promise.'

'Artaynte is right, my angel. Remember, you could become Queen.'

Hadasseh looked at her cousin with sadness in her big eyes. 'I somehow did not expect you to take her side in this matter.'

'I am not taking anyone's side, Hadasseh; I am simply being realistic. The two of you cannot keep hiding away here for the rest of your lives, hoping no-one will recognise you. If you were to marry the King, you would not have to do that anymore and neither would Artaynte. No-one then would dare harm the Queen of the Persians nor her Maid of Honour.'

'But there will be many concubines and princesses. What if I am not chosen? How could I spend the rest of my life at the beck and call of a man who wants me for just one thing and one thing only. It is humiliating.'

'What if I could guarantee that you will become Queen?' said Artaynte quietly.

'How could that be? The matter is not up to you.'

'No, you are right. But it is up to Hegai.'

Hadasseh spun around. 'What?'

'Hegai has been entrusted with choosing and preparing the concubines for the King. You and I both know that, given the choice, he will select you as concubine. I also know that when you are presented to the King, he will choose you as his Queen.'

'How can you know all this?'

Her friend tapped the side of her long nose. 'Leave it to Artaynte. Artaynte knows everything.'

THE King stood on the coast and watched as his army slowly crossed the mile-wide stretch of water separating Asia from Europe. If the Greeks had any kind of gumption, it was then that they would have attacked, while his army was at its most vulnerable. There had been considerable delay due to the fact that the first pontoon bridge had been swept away during a freak storm and now, as he watched, the ships stood off in case the same thing happened again.

Artabazanes rode up. 'We are ready, my Lord King.'

'Very well, my brother.' He turned to his advisor. 'Come Haman, see Greece at last.'

'I am weary, your Majesty. The long march has been hard on us all.'

The King pointed. 'You see those hills on the other side of the water? That is Thrace. Beyond that is Macedonia and Thessaly. In a few weeks, come what may, you and I will be in Athens.'

'I feel unhappy, Sire. I wish I was more convinced that we are doing the right thing.'

'It was you who cast the lots which guided us here. Therefore, it is the will of Ahura-Mazda. We cannot fail.'

'As you say, my Lord King. I am with you unto death.'

MORDECAI watched as Artaynte put the finishing touches to his cousin's hair. 'You will remember what I have said.'

'Of course, my father.'

'From now on, you must forget the name Hadasseh. You must always be Astur of Babylon and I must be called Marduka at all times.'

'Will I not be able to speak with you?'

'Not for the time being. There are many who suspect that I am a Jew though, so far, I have been able to overcome the matter. However, if anyone finds out that you are one, too, it could be the end for us all. Artaynte must become our go-between each week.'

'Then we will keep in touch?'

'Of course, my child. One day, we may be able to meet openly but that day is far away.'

Hadasseh smiled a little. 'I trust your judgement, my father.'

THROUGHOUT that summer, news reports came in regularly and the latest from the western front was the subject of most discussions at Shushan.

'I hear that the King has marched unhindered into Aetolia,' said Artaynte as she gently smoothed oil of Myrrh into Astur's back.

'Is that good?' asked Astur, not having the faintest idea where the place was.

'It means that the whole army has crossed the Hellespont safely and that they have penetrated right through Thessaly.'

'What of the fleet?' asked Astur, her eyes closed as a young girl trimmed her toenails and smoothed oil into her ankles and soles.

'Hegai said that the fleet has sailed through a canal the King had dug across the Acte Peninsula to avoid the terrible winds and waves which destroyed his father's fleet off Mount Athos.'

'So all is going well?'

'It would seem so.' Artaynte playfully slapped her friend's bare bottom. 'Turn over.'

Astur sighed as she rolled over. 'Must I go through all this?'

'Yes, you must, and stop complaining. It is traditional that, before any maiden can be admitted to the King, she must be massaged for a year with oil of myrrh and balsam oil. She has to have skin as soft as a baby's bottom.'

Astur squealed as Artaynte splashed some cool oil onto her chest. 'That's cold.'

'Look, if you don't stop bellyaching, I will get Hegai in here and you know what he is like. He won't let you get away with all this moaning and groaning.'

Astur pulled a face. 'You're worse than Marduka ever was, you are.'

'It is for your own good. You want to look your best for the King don't you?'

'Of course, but...'

'Then lie still and enjoy it while you can.' Artaynte stood up. 'Here, let Melane take over for a while, my back is killing me.'

'Who's complaining now?' muttered Astur with a sly grin.

'Hmm!' said Artaynte, her hands on her hips. 'Right girls, what do we do with someone who complains?'

Astur instantly sat up. 'You wouldn't!'

'Oh yes we would. Grab her arms and legs, girls.'

Astur screamed as Artaynte and the other maids she had been assigned grabbed her wrists and ankles and lifted her bodily from the couch.

'Put me down,' she yelled, kicking and struggling in vain.

'One, two, three,' said Artaynte as they swung the screaming girl backwards and forwards until, with a shout, they pitched her into the bathing pool with a mighty splash.

'What girls do?' called the booming voice from the curtained doorway and the room fell silent. 'Hurt Astur and I very unhappy.'

'It's all right, Hegai,' called Astur as she shook the water from her face. 'I was teasing them.'

He pointed an accusing finger at her. 'If you get hurt, you no good to King, and King make angry with Hegai. Hegai then banished to Kavir and Hegai not like that.'

'I said we were sorry. We don't want you sent to the salt-wastes.'

'Then you must do as told. Is very important.'

'Hegai,' said Astur as she stepped from the pool. 'From now on, we will do just as you say. You have been very good to me, bringing me here to the best part of the Palace. We don't want to spoil it after all you have done.'

'Then behave self.' He suddenly smiled. 'When you Queen, you tell Hegai what to do.'

'When I am Queen,' said Astur with a sly grin. 'I will make your life a misery like you have mine these last weeks. Eat this, eat that, drink this, drink that. I'm about sick of fruit and vegetables.'

'They good for you.'

'That's what my mother used to say.'

'Do not mock mother. Mother in land of gods.'

Astur sighed. 'I wasn't mocking, Hegai. I'm just so bored with so little to do but lie here and be pampered.'

'Very well. Tomorrow, you run round palace seven times.'

'Run? Seven times? That'll kill me.'

'Seven times. Before breakfast. No run, no food.'

'All the other concubines don't have to do that, do they?'

'Other girls not going to be Queen. Up early, run. Hegai has spoken.'

He left.

'Now look what you've done,' said Astur accusingly.

'Me?' said Artaynte innocently. 'What did I do?'

'You got me into this, Artaynte, so you had better be up early too. Remember? Seven times around the palace.' She stuck out her bare chest in imitation of the eunuch. 'No run, no food.'

KHSHAYARSHA'S army came unstuck at Thermopylae. After having driven back the Greeks during a minor skirmish at Themes, the Spartans dug themselves in to hold the pass against the massive Persian army.

'Why can we not break through?' demanded the King.

'The pass is too narrow, your Majesty,' said his older brother.

'There has to be a way around them, Artabazanes. We have been here two days and have lost thousands of men while they sit and throw rocks at us from the hills.'

'I will make enquiries of our Macedonian allies.'

'You do that, my brother. I do not intend to stay here much longer. The fleet is vulnerable without our keeping up on land.'

'It shall be done, my Lord King.' He rode off.

The King turned to the old man beside him. 'Well, Haman. What do the gods say now?'

Haman sat cross-legged on the ground and cast lots. After considerable meditation as to the meaning, he lifted his head. 'Mithra says that tomorrow we shall destroy them all and take the pass.'

Khshayarsha looked at the Magi long and hard. To even question the gods at this stage of a battle would not only be foolish but also disheartening to the troops.

'Very well.' He turned to his brother-in-law. 'Mardonius, tell the other generals. We break through tomorrow. I know yet not how, but Ahura-Mazda has spoken and we shall obey.'

THE news spread through the city like wildfire and parties were held long into the night.

'Tonight,' said Hegai. 'Special treat for my girls. I have instructed wine to come for you all.'

'Wine?' said Artaynte with excitement. 'Whoopee!'

'How long will it be before the King returns?' asked Astur seriously.

'News take two weeks to arrive. By now, King in Athens. If

all go well, he be home by winter.'

'I see.'

Hegai placed his hand gently under her chin and lifted it. 'You not be sad. When King come, you be very happy, wait and see.'

She shrugged. 'I just can't believe all this is happening to me.'

'You believe,' he said with a smile. 'By spring, you be Queen. Hegai know.'

Astur returned his smile. 'I trust you, Hegai.'

He patted her gently on the shoulder. 'You good girl. King like good girl. You not at all like Amestris.'

'I only saw her once. Was she always like that?'

'Her father let her get like that. King always busy, not notice much. When King insist, she disobey. Amestris bad Queen.'

'I hope I don't become like that.'

He shook his head. 'No. You different.'

'How can I be sure I am doing and saying the right things?'

'You do just as always. No try to be different. Act normal.' He smiled. 'King like that.'

'The King liked Artaynte didn't he?'

Hegai wagged his finger. 'No. King love Artaynte. Is not same.'

'Will he love me, Hegai?'

'If he don't, Khshayarsha pretty stupid King. Me love you as own child.'

Astur laughed. 'You are a eunuch. You don't have any children.'

'If I do, you are she.'

She threw her arms around the giant. 'I love you, Hegai.'

THE King watched with sadness as the smoke rose over the city of Athens. He had not wanted it to be this way but some of his generals had become over-zealous. Fortunately for the inhabitants of the city, the Greek General, Themistocles, had persuaded most of the populous to flee to the islands where they would be safe. Greece had fallen to Persia, but at what cost? Athens had been taken but the fleet had been decimated at Salamis. In trying to chase the Greeks into the narrow channel, the Persian fleet had been trapped by the easier-to-manoeuvre Greek Triremes. For the first time in many years, Khshayarsha felt sad. His brother and brother-in-law were still there and, in spite of all their differences and rivalries, they had fought well, side-by-side. But now, could they govern what they had taken as well as they had battled for it?

He turned to his attendants. 'I am ready. Call the generals for a council of war. In one week, I leave for Persia.'

HADASSEH trembled as Melane finished brushing her hair. Looking at herself in the polished bronze mirror, she saw the reflection of a girl who looked little more than twelve years old. Unlike the concubines who had preceded her into the King's presence, she wore no make-up of any kind, no flowers in her hair, no expensive perfume from the East. Hegai nodded his approval and bade her stand.

'Are you sure this is right?' she said quietly. 'Haman's daughter looked really beautiful last night and she was not chosen.'

'Is perfect,' said the giant. 'After all years with King, Hegai know what pleases Khshayarsha.'

Hadasseh spun herself around on her bare feet and her simple skirt swung out like a dancing dress. The weeks of exercise around the palace gardens had given her a leanness and fitness which clearly showed as her eyes sparkled with health and her long black hair shone with vitality.

'Is tonight,' said Hegai. 'Artaynte teach you how to prevent pain when first time with man?'

Hadasseh nodded but had a sudden mental picture of her young mother being repeatedly raped by a group of half-drunken soldiers while her father lay dying on the ground. Sarah had dared to be a Jewess and that had meant open sport, and the nightmare flooded back to her despite her continued efforts to forget. Hadasseh groaned at the memory and only the arms of Artaynte calmed her back to the present.

'Remember what I told you?'

Hadasseh nodded as her friend gently wiped away the tears.

'You are seventh to be presented to King,' said Hegai. 'You are also last.'

Hadasseh looked up sharply. 'But there are a dozen others after me. The King will want to test them all before making his final decision.'

The giant smiled. 'Trust Hegai. Hegai know King. You are last. I go now to prepare for great banquet I am certain King will order.'

'You seem very sure,' said the nervous Hadasseh.

'I, too, am sure,' said Artaynte. She smiled. 'Ready?'

The young woman nodded and held her head high. 'I am ready.'

KHSHAYARSHA lay on his couch in the innermost room as his attendants laid out food on the low tables.

'Which concubine is it tonight, Harbona?'

The servant bowed. 'It is a young maiden from Babylon,

Your Highness.'

'Very well,' he sighed, remembering how his last Chaldean queen had turned out. 'Show her in.'

'It shall be done, my Lord King.'

The attendant backed from the room and, shortly afterwards, a young fair-haired woman walked slowly in.

The King's eyes lit up for a moment as he swung his legs from the couch. 'Artaynte, I did not expect to see you again. You shouldn't be here.'

'I had to come, my Lord King. I have a brought a present for you.'

'A present? Be quick, my child. If you are seen here, I shall have to have you executed. You have been banished from the palace upon pain of death. I will have no option despite my deep love for you.'

'I am not here as concubine, Sire. Before I give you my present, I claim my right to become Maid of Honour to the new Queen.'

'Artaynte,' said the King. 'That promise was conditional upon you finding the girl from the river.'

The young woman's eyes sparkled as she smiled. 'So it was. Allow me to present to you my best friend, Princess Astur of Babylon.'

She stepped to one side and the King's eyes lifted slowly to the doorway. He neither saw nor heard Artaynte leave and he stood, his mouth open, as the young girl walked slowly towards him.

'The girl from the river,' he breathed as his heart-beat raced.

'Your Majesty,' said Astur as she curtsied to the floor.

The King took her hand and lifted her to her feet. 'Is it really you?'

'It is, my Lord King.'

'You haven't changed a bit.'

She smiled. 'You flatter me, your Majesty.'

'May I touch you?' asked the King, wondering why on earth he was being so polite.

A slight tremor ran through Hadasseh as she anticipated the next hour and the King was quick to realise the reason why that might be. 'Do not be afraid. I will not harm you.'

With a final swallow, Hadasseh smiled and stepped forward into the King's arms. For several minutes, Khshayarsha held her tight until the tremors ceased and then kissed her forehead gently. 'Now I have found you again, I find that I want to keep you just as you are.'

'My Lord King,' said the surprised Hadasseh. 'I am yours to do as you wish.'

Khshayarsha looked at her long and hard. Her dark hair shone in the light of the oil lamps and her face glowed with health. 'You know what I wish?'

Astur looked into his eyes. 'What you wish is what I wish. May it always be so.'

'I wish you to become my Queen.'

'B..but...' she stammered. 'You don't yet know whether I am suitable.'

'You are eminently suitable, that I already know.' The King turned and clapped his hands. Harbona rushed in.

'A banquet,' called the King, raising his arms. 'A banquet for the people of Shushan. Proclaim an amnesty throughout the realm, from India to Ethiopia. All political prisoners are freed, national debts are cancelled. Let gifts go to all satraps and princes of the Empire. Tonight, Persia has a new Queen.'

The servant was flabbergasted at the suddenness of the decision. 'A new Queen, My Lord King?'

'Yes.' He took Astur's hand. 'Let a message be sent to the

length and breadth of the inhabited earth. Princess Astur of Babylon has become Queen of the Persians.'

THREE men were not celebrating. Expecting the decision concerning the choosing of the queen to be delayed for at least another two weeks, they had been caught unprepared.

'Teresh. It must be tonight,' said the tall one.

'But it is the wedding night, the King and Queen will be well-guarded.'

'Am I not Commander of the Guard? The King has chosen his Queen and will want to be alone with her so the guards will understand if they are withdrawn from the area surrounding the king's chambers. There will never be another opportunity when they are so vulnerable.'

'So be it. Bigthana and I will see to the matter personally.'

'Remember. Do not kill the Queen. She must be saved for the people who will then be able to watch for themselves as justice is carried out.'

'It shall be as you command, my Lord Artabanus.'

MORDECAI raised himself from his hands and knees in the narrow passageway above the gateway. He had not heard all of the conversation which had taken place in the opposite turret, nor had he identified all the plotters but of one thing he was certain - whoever they were, these men intended to kill the King and his cousin was to take the blame for the deed. Quietly, he made his way along the passage in the dark and hurried down his own stairs. Pausing at the door to make sure all was clear, he then slipped through the shadows towards the palace where the festivities were already beginning to wane. At the gate, he saw a familiar figure.

'Melane,' he whispered. 'Are either Artaynte or Hegai about?'

'I don't know,' she said, already a little merry from the wine.

'I must find her, and quickly.'

'Why? It's time to dance.' She put her arms around his neck. 'Dance with me, Marduka.'

He pushed her away. 'I must find Artaynte. Someone intends to kill the King tonight.'

'Don't be silly. The King is to be with Astur tonight.' She leant closer conspiratorially and giggled. 'He is going to make love to her.'

'We must stop them.'

'Stop them? You should have seen Astur at the banquet. She couldn't stop staring at the King with her big eyes. They are in love.'

'But don't you realise? There is a plot to kill them both. I must find Hegai or Artaynte.'

'I might know where they are,' Melane said with a wink.

'Then fetch them, girl. Quickly.'

'All right, all right. There's no need to shout.'

Ten minutes later, Artaynte appeared and grabbed Marduka's arm. 'What is this Melane is mumbling about a plot to kill the King?'

'Thank goodness someone believes me. I overheard some men plotting near the gatehouse. They plan to murder the King tonight and place the blame upon Astur.'

'Then we must stop them.'

'Better still, we must catch them in the act. If I call out the guard, can you make sure that Astur is aware?'

'Of course,' said Artaynte. 'Leave it to me.'

She ran through the palace garden, frantically looking for Astur. For some strange reason, she thought as she ran, there were no guards to be found anywhere in the main palace complex. Freely, she wandered in and out of the chambers until she came to the King's rooms. Her heart was in her mouth as she tiptoed towards the King's own chamber and tapped on the wall, praying she was not too late. A man opened the curtains.

She sighed with relief. 'Thank goodness it is you, Harbona. There is a plot against the King. We must protect him.'

'A plot? Don't be ridiculous. The palace is well guarded.'

'Then how do you think I got this far? I tell you I have seen no-one in the palace.'

Harbona stuck his head out into the empty passageway and confirmed her truthful words.

'Come inside,' he said quickly and Artaynte followed him into the anti-room, suddenly wondering if Harbona was in on the plot. If he was, she had just made the last mistake of her life.

Harbona knocked on the far doorway and opened the curtain carefully. 'My Lord King. Forgive me but it is an emergency. There is a plot against your life.'

The King strode to the door and saw Artaynte. 'Who is in the palace?'

'The guards are all away from their posts,' confirmed the Maid of Honour. 'There is no-one.'

'Very well. Harbona, who is there in the chambers?'

'Just ourselves, my Lord King. It was as you commanded.'

'What is it?' said the voice and Astur came to the door.

'Harbona, look after the Queen,' said the King. 'We will get to the bottom of this matter.' He suddenly had inspiration. 'Artaynte, run to the court of women. See who is left who might help us.'

She bowed. 'It is done, Your Majesty.'

Artaynte ran off down the passage as Harbona guided Astur to the bed where he bade her lie.

The King took his attendant to one side. 'What weapons do we have?'

'None, your Majesty. Weapons are banned from the central palace area by order of the Commander of the Guard.' Harbona stiffened. 'There are footsteps.'

Together, they backed into a curtained alcove off the antiroom and waited. Slowly, the door creaked open and two shadows entered. The King and attendant watched as they crept stealthily towards the King's chamber. Astur called out as the door opened and the King stepped forward to help. The men turned and saw him and one raised his spear to throw. Suddenly, Khshayarsha was thrust aside as a giant burst into the room and rushed towards the men. A great scuffle broke out in the darkness as Artaynte shouted in the passageway outside and figures started to appear in the distance. Within minutes, the room was full of people and the two men were lying on the floor as Hegai stumbled to his feet, the spear which had been intended for the King protruding from his chest.

'Hegai!' screamed Astur and threw her arms around him as he fell to his knees. 'Artaynte, get help, quickly.'

'Is too late,' sighed the giant. 'I dead.'

'Not yet, you're not.' Taking control, she looked up at Harbona. 'Where's that healer? Fetch him quickly.'

Guards arrived into the mêlée and among them, Artabanus, looking very ill indeed. Astur watched as he entered and was a little surprised at the expression upon his face.

'Where were you when I needed you?' bellowed the King and his uncle made some lame excuse as the guards arrested Bigthana and Teresh. 'Take them away. In the morning, I want to look out of my window and see them hanging in the public square.'

Artabanus nodded and, still looking sick, left.

'Harbona,' continued the King. 'I want a full report of this incident. Investigate it fully and see that it is written into the official records.'

Harbona bowed. 'It shall be done, my Lord King.'

'Artaynte,' said Astur quietly as the men took the giant away. 'Will you look after Hegai?'

'Of course. I will remain with him until morning.'

'Thank you.'

The King closed the curtain and they were alone. 'I will understand if you wish to return to your own quarters.'

The Queen of the Persians smiled a little. 'You are most kind, my Lord King. However, alone, I will fret for Hegai. Tonight, I need comfort in the arms of the one I love.'

THE giant Hegai died during the night. The man who had bravely jumped into the raging waters of the Choaspes, who had befriended Hadasseh and Artaynte, who had made an orphan into a queen, had died saving the life of his King. The whole of Shushan was in mourning the next day as the King commanded his body to be carried throughout the city in state. Artaynte and Marduka stood side-by-side at the palace gate as his body was carried through.

'How is Astur taking it?' asked Marduka.

'She is surprisingly calm and collected. I think I may have underestimated my friend.'

'That I have often done. What news of the assassination attempt?'

'The men were caught and sentenced by the King. Their

bodies were hung up in the public square this morning for all to see. I do not think the King is too happy with Artabanus. He left the palace unprotected.'

'That's odd,' said Mordecai thoughtfully. 'One of the men I overheard plotting murmured something about the guard being withdrawn. I didn't hear all that was said but I got that bit. Maybe Bigthana and Teresh had found out the guard would be light.'

The Princess smirked. 'Or perhaps Artabanus knew they were coming and deliberately withdrew the guard.'

Mordecai turned on her sharply. 'Artaynte, do you know what you are saying? You are inferring that Artabanus would murder his own nephew.'

'But surely, if the King was to die, he would become ruler himself. The King's own sons are too young and have been well cocooned from the intrigues, and Artabazanes is far away in Thrace. It would have been a perfect time for Artabanus to be found in charge.'

'Whatever you do, do not let anyone at the palace hear you speaking such words. If what you have suggested ever got back to the King...?'

'Do not fear, Marduka. I may be young but I am not that stupid.' She looked at the last of the train and sighed. 'I must return to Astur.'

'Give her my love.'

Artaynte kissed his cheek. 'I will.'

AT the end of the mourning for Hegai and the celebrations over the new Queen, Khshayarsha sat with her in the interior room of the palace area.

'I must go away for a few weeks,' he said as they ate. 'I need to go to Persepolis to see how my new palace is coming along. It must be finished for the New Year celebrations. Also, I wish for time to meditate.'

'You have decisions to make?'

'I must decide what to do about the Greeks. I fear that Mardonius and Artabazanes will end up fighting one another unless I make more permanent arrangements.'

'**They** tell me that Megabyzus is eager to please you now that he has become your son-in-law. Surely either he or Artabanus could relieve one or the other of them and thus reduce the possibility of rivalry.'

'You are right, my dear. Do you know? It is most refreshing to be able to discuss such matters with a Queen who is not only beautiful in form but also highly intelligent.'

Astur blushed. 'You flatter me, my Lord King.'

'Not so. For the first time in my reign, I am content to leave Shushan knowing my people are in good hands.'

'One day, I should like to see this city your father started and you are now in the process of finishing.'

'At the new year, I shall take you there. You will sit beside me on a throne of gold and the satraps of all the nations must come, do obeisance before me and swear allegiance to my Queen.'

'I shall look forward to seeing the fruits of your hard work and to meeting your subjects from afar.'

'You will see to the matter of the harem while I am away?'

'It shall be done, my Lord King. I just hope you will be pleased with my choice.'

'You are Queen, Astur. Whatever you decide will be commanded by royal decree.'

'When do you leave?'

'I leave tomorrow.'

'Have I pleased you enough so you will grant me one request

before you leave?'

'Anything. Up to half of my kingdom.'

Astur smiled. 'I ask for neither gold nor power. I request just one small favour on your last night in Shushan.'

'Name it and it shall be yours.'

'I offer you Artaynte as concubine and ask that you re-affirm your love for her as you have loved me.'

Khshayarsha smiled and touched her face gently. As King it was his right to choose whichever queen or concubine he fancied and they both knew it. However, this was the first queen who, seemingly, understood his needs.

'It is my wish.' He paused. 'Do you know? I think that you and I are going get along just fine.'

Astur smiled a wry smile. 'My Lord King, I would stake my life on it.'

ASTUR settled down well at the palace. She was kind to all who came to see her yet not soft when deputising for the King. As a result, her courtiers came to have a great respect for her and her word became not only truth but law. The palace was quiet without the King but Astur was busy. The sad death of Hegai had provided a vacancy in the supervision of the Harem and she wanted to find someone who was not only suitable but also a eunuch who would serve the King's best interests. It was her first real assignment at the palace and she was determined to please her husband and king. In the end, she had sent Artaynte to ask the advice of Marduka who had recommended a certain Asian who now stood before her.

'How old are you, Hathach?' she asked kindly but firmly, trying her best to sound like a queen.

'I am twenty-two, Your Majesty.'

'And you are the son of Yorman of Bactria?'

'It is so.'

'How long have you been with the King?'

'For two years, your Majesty. I was chosen as junior eunuch for the King's concubines at Ecbatana.'

'Very well. I will appoint you on one condition.'

'Anything, Your Majesty.'

'You will report directly to myself. I want to know everything that goes on among the concubines. Everything. Do you understand?'

'I do, Your Majesty.'

'You know Princess Artaynte?'

He nodded.

'You will also keep in contact with her. If it is not possible to get in touch with me personally at any time, you may speak with Artaynte. Artaynte and I are as one. Do I make myself quite clear?'

He looked puzzled but nodded again.

She smiled at him. 'Welcome to my harem.'

'You mean I have the job?'

'Of course. However, failure to please me at any time will result in the King's wrath.'

'I will do exactly as you say, your Majesty.'

Astur clapped her hands and the attendant appeared. 'Ah, Harbona. Hathach has become our new chief eunuch. Please show him to his quarters.'

Harbona bowed. 'As you command, my Queen.'

'And would you send Artaynte to me, please.'

'At once, your Majesty.'

Astur slipped from the throne and went to the window from where she could see right across the palace garden. It seemed so peaceful at the moment but, she knew, it was misleading.

Somewhere to the east, Khshayarsha was at Persepolis, supervising the construction of the new banqueting hall which was due to be finished in time for the New Year celebrations. Away to the north and west, Artabazanes and Mardonius were struggling to hold onto the territory gained in Greece. With each report came news of growing unrest among the peoples of Athenia and Macedonia who strongly resented the Persian occupation of their hereditary lands. It was an uneasy peace.

A slight noise made her turn. 'Princess Artaynte is not in her chamber, your Majesty. Shall I send servants to look for her?'

Astur frowned. It was unlike her friend to depart without leaving a message. Not only that but, upon reflection, Astur had not seen her all morning. 'Send Artabanus to me.'

After several minutes delay, the Commander of the Guard strode in, ill-disguised contempt upon his face. 'You wished to see me?'

She turned to face him, controlling her feelings at his impudence. 'I did, Lord Artabanus. I need a search made of the palace. I want you to find Princess Artaynte.

His face broke into a leer. 'You want the Palace Guard to go looking for some girl?'

'I will remind you, Lord Artabanus,' she said evenly, 'Princess Artaynte is not just "some girl" as you have called her. She is the King's concubine and my own Maid of Honour.'

'Oh yes,' he sneered. 'I had forgotten.'

'You don't like me, do you?'

'With respect,' he said without showing any. 'You are not of Achaemenid blood. You have no right to the throne of Persia.'

'And you have, I suppose?'

'I am brother of Darius the Great.'

'It would be as well that you do not let the King hear you

speak as you do now.'

'Khshayarsha knows how I feel.'

'And he tolerates you? I fear that if I were he, I would have you banished to the Kavir for your impudence.'

Astur had never once raised her voice during the conversation, her words coming clearly and evenly. Artabanus turned towards her and, after a few moments, failed to meet her stare. 'You dare to threaten me?'

'I speak in the King's name, Artabanus. What he wishes is what I wish. If any harm has befallen Artaynte, woe betide you when he returns.'

The return of Harbona disturbed their friendly conversation. 'Your Majesty, we have found the Princess. She is...unwell.'

Astur's heart skipped a beat. 'Where is she?'

'She is at the house of Marduka the gatekeeper.'

Astur frowned. Why had Artaynte gone to see Mordecai? She made up her mind. 'I will go to see her there.'

Harbona looked astounded. 'You are Queen, you cannot leave the palace.'

'Nonsense. Lord Artabanus is the Commander of the Guard. He will accompany me.'

'It is most unusual, Your Majesty.'

Astur winked at him. 'Harbona, I am most unusual. You should know that by now.'

Harbona was not going to fall into that trap. It was more than his head was worth.

'Come, Artabanus,' said the Queen of the Persians and strode from the room.

The sun outside was hot on her face as Astur walked across the marble courtyard and, despite the look of astonishment on the guards' faces, she walked straight out into the streets of Shushan. Artabanus smiled to himself as he followed, not too closely. Perhaps in the crowd there was someone who was currently dissatisfied with Khshayarsha's rule; perhaps angry enough to make an attempt on the Queen's life. Maybe she would be kidnapped by extremists and held to ransom, tortured maybe. In his mind, he could hear her screams of agony and almost allowed himself a titter. Gradually, he and his companions began to drop back a little to allow opportunity for such an eventuality and felt a wave of pleasure wash over him as several in the crowd rushed towards their Queen. He was dismayed when, instead of attacking her, they threw themselves at her feet and began to do obeisance to her. His dismay turned to anger when, instead of chastising them for their lack of dignity in her presence, Astur smiled to them and bade them stand, touching them and wishing them well. By the time she reached Marduka's gatehouse, she had quite a following of people and the face of Artabanus was as black as thunder.

The Queen swept into the gatehouse and Marduka gaped as she pushed past him and up the stairs. At the top, she paused while her eyes adjusted to the dim light and then stepped softly towards the bed where her friend lay sleeping. Astur sat down and gently touched Artaynte's forehead. There was no fever.

She heard Mordecai enter behind her. 'What is wrong with her?'

'She has been hurt,' he said quietly.

'Hurt? How? Where?'

'She was coming to see me last night. When it turned sunset, I left the guards in charge and went to look for her. I found her near the city wall.'

'So? What is wrong with her?'

Mordecai didn't answer so Astur turned to face him and he looked at the floor. A tear trickled down his face. Astur held her breath. She had never seen a man cry before and certainly not her cousin.

She stood up before him and held him tight. 'What is it, my father?'

'Artaynte...,' he swallowed. 'Artaynte has...' He looked up at her. 'Artaynte has been raped.'

Astur felt as though a great dagger had been thrust into her belly and was twisting and turning inside her, cutting her inward parts into tiny pieces. A vision of her mother flashed into her mind and of men laughing at the blood all over her legs. She clenched her teeth. 'Who did this evil deed?'

Mordecai stood silent with head bowed.

'Who?' she demanded, grabbing him by the cloak.

'I...'

She shook her cousin. 'Who?'

'Sataspes. Artaynte told me when I found her.'

Astur said nothing for several minutes. 'Can she be moved?'

Mordecai nodded. 'I think so. There are no broken bones, just bruises.'

'Any blood?'

'No, no blood. Just the pain inside, she said.'

'Right,' Astur said, letting go of him. 'I shall send the healer immediately and people to carry her to the palace.'

Mordecai grabbed her arm. 'Wait. What will you do?'

'I will have Sataspes executed.'

'Don't do anything rash, my child.'

'Rash?' she spat, barely in control of herself. 'When I am through with these people, they will wish they had pleaded with Khshayarsha to retain Amestris as Queen.'

Gritting her teeth, Astur stormed down the stairs out into the harsh glare of day and muttering crowds. She passed a baffled Artabanus. 'I want you at the palace immediately. And bring that worthless son of yours with you.'

'But...' he began.

She turned suddenly. 'At once!'

There was something in her eyes which brought a flash of fear to his heart as he simply nodded and then watched her storm towards the palace, the crowd behind her. Astur burst into the palace and summoned the guard. With a dozen Immortals in tow, the Queen gathered a scribe and several attendants and, entering the inner sanctuary, sat on the golden throne. Gradually, her heartbeat returned to normal as the men stood around her respectfully; all of them wondering what was going to happen but none of them daring to be the one to ask.

Harbona entered. 'Lords Artabanus and Sataspes to see you, your Majesty.'

'Show them in. And stay.'

'Very well,' he bowed and stepped aside to allow the Commander of the Guard to enter accompanied by a young man of about twenty-five. They stopped before her but did not bow. The soldiers grew fidgety.

'Sataspes,' she called and the young man stepped forward looking guilty. 'Where were you last evening?'

'I was with friends,' he said quietly.

'Why did you assault my Maid of Honour?'

Pandemonium broke out. Artabanus started to bluster while Harbona asked the Queen if she was well. The young man simply stared at the floor. The room gradually fell silent again. 'Well?'

'I...' began Sataspes.

'Don't answer her,' said his father. 'The Queen has no right to hold Court in the King's absence.'

'I speak in the name of the King.' She dropped her voice and stared at the young man. 'Well?'

'I was drunk, Your Majesty.'

'And that gave you the right to take the King's concubine and assault her?'

'No, your Majesty. I regret my action.'

Astur gradually calmed down.

'I must protest,' shouted Artabanus. 'You have no right.'

Astur looked straight at Artabanus but spoke to the guards. 'Arrest Sataspes and throw him into the prison.'

The guards hesitated for a moment then two stepped forward.

'Stop!' commanded Artabanus. 'I am in charge of the Palace Guard. No-one gives orders but myself.' He turned to face them. 'You are dismissed. Go to your quarters.'

They hesitated once more and one or two bowed their heads and made for the door.

Astur didn't move but calmly stated; 'Any man who leaves this room will join Sataspes in prison.'

The guards were clearly confused as to whether to obey the Commander who they had been trained to follow without question, or this Queen whom they hardly knew.

Astur stepped from the throne. 'It is the law of the Achaemenids that rape is not permitted within the boundaries of the city nor outside within peacetime. The punishment for such a crime is death.' She turned on Artabanus. 'I understand that you were with the King when he made the decree after the rape and murder of my own mother. I will not by-pass the law simply because the lawbreaker happens to be your son.' Astur walked up to Sataspes who shook with terror. 'What say you, Sataspes?'

The young man bowed his head. 'It is as you wish, my Queen.'

Artabanus intervened once more. 'They were but boys

having fun.'

'Fun?' said Astur, whirling around. 'Is that how you get your fun, my Lord Artabanus? If it had not been for Sataspes apparent sorrow over the matter, I would have had him executed without delay.'

'I will not have my son imprisoned for simply using a concubine.'

Astur stepped close to him, her face but inches from his. 'Princess Artaynte is not just any concubine, Artabanus. She is the King's favourite. And when he hears of this, he will spare no mercy.'

'I protest...'

'Don't bother. Artabanus of the Achaemenids, you are hereby removed from your position as Commander of the Guard.'

'You cannot do that,' he blustered.

'I just did. And one more word and I will have you imprisoned with your son.'

Artabanus opened his mouth to speak but, seeing the look on her face and the soldiers who were clearly ready to obey her, he closed it again and turned on his heel and left the palace.

'Guards,' said Astur quietly. 'Imprison Sataspes in his own quarters. See that he is well provided for until the King returns from Persepolis and makes the final judgement. If any try to see him or release him, throw them into the deepest dungeons.'

The Sergeant-at-Arms bowed. 'At your command, Highness.'

She smiled at him. 'Thank you.'

He left to do his duty. The normally-subdued Harbona allowed a trace of a smile to cross his lips and was not quite quick enough at removing it before he found Astur watching him.

'With respect, your Majesty,' he said quickly, 'That was close.'

'It was wasn't it?' she said and sat down on the marble steps beside the throne. 'Tell me. Is Megabyzus back from Babylon yet?'

'He arrived yesterday, your Majesty.'

'Please send him to me immediately.'

Harbona bowed. 'It shall be as you have spoken.'

While she waited, Astur toyed with the hem of her red and white dress and with her innermost feelings. Had she done the right thing? To overlook the incident would have undermined the King's authority and caused many to feel that adverse justice was good only for the poor. However, in removing Artabanus from his post, she had made an enemy at a time when she needed friends in high places. Harbona showed Megabyzus into the room and the son-in-law of the King stood, respectfully, as Astur got to her feet and faced him.

'You have subdued Babylon?'

'Most effectively, your Majesty. It was necessary to melt down the great statue of Marduk in the city and desecrate a few temples but, in the end, they know who is in charge.'

She slowly walked round the young Prince. 'Who is in charge, Megabyzus?'

'Why, Khshayarsha the King of course.'

'Are you certain?'

'He is King of Kings and Lord of Lords, second only to Lord Ahura-Mazda.'

Astur relaxed. 'You have served the King well. I wish to reward your bravery.'

'Your word is my command.'

'You are hereby appointed Commander of the Palace Guard. When Khshayarsha returns, he will either confirm or overrule your commission.'

'But, Artabanus...'

'..Is no longer in a position of trust.'

He stood and reflected for a moment and then, realising the possibilities if he played his cards right, bowed before Astur. 'It shall be as you command, your Majesty.'

'Your first assignment will be to issue a decree. The King has already spoken the law and it has been so written. Any man of the Empire of Persia who proceeds to rape a girl or woman in Shushan the Castle or outside the city in peacetime is to be publicly dismembered and his house turned into a public privy. The law has been spoken, so let it be done.'

KHSHAYARSHA returned a month later, full of the progress which had been made at Persepolis. He was not alone. With him were two young men of about Astur's own age.

'My Lord King,' the Queen greeted at the main gate of the Palace. 'Welcome home.'

He stood before her and held her shoulders. 'It is good to be back, Astur. I have missed you.'

She smiled at the compliment. 'With your permission, I have arranged a great banquet for my Lord and King.'

Khshayarsha was more than a little taken aback at such an unexpected greeting. 'I would be honoured, my Queen.' He gestured towards the young men who rode on horseback behind his throne carriage. 'These are my sons, Darius and Artakhshayarsha.'

Astur smiled up at them and the older one nodded slightly while the younger came as close to ignoring her as was possible. She bowed before them. 'I am honoured to welcome you to Shushan, My Lords. You will also be most welcome at my banquet.'

Darius actually smiled at the invitation whereas his younger brother produced something more akin to a scowl.

Khshayarsha took Astur's arm and they walked together up the marble staircase. 'I noticed that it was Megabyzus that met me on the road. I didn't like to ask but is my uncle unwell?'

'Artabanus is perfectly well, my Lord King. He has asked to see you during the banquet.'

Khshayarsha was intrigued but asked no more as they went their respective ways to prepare themselves for the meal.

Astur had excelled, having personally instructed the royal kitchens and staff and sent post-riders to Caspia for sturgeon's eggs and to the Plains of Sharon for fresh oranges. It was the very best meal Khshayarsha had ever tasted and he reclined alongside his Queen and sons until Artabanus strode in to beg an attendance. For a long time, the two men spoke in whispers and, occasionally, one or the other of them looked in Astur's direction.

Eventually, the King called for silence. 'It has been brought to my attention what has been done in my absence and I am most distressed.'

The King was looking straight at Astur as he spoke and Artabanus looked on with ill-disguised glee. Astur hung her head in shame as she felt the eyes of everyone upon her and to be brought so much embarrassment in front of the King was more than she could take.

The King turned his head. 'Lord Artabanus. Go and fetch Sataspes and bring him to me.'

Artabanus left, the beaming smile of vindication all over his face.

The King leaned closer to Astur. 'Why?'

'Because he broke your express command and raped my Maid of Honour.'

'Where is Artaynte now? Has she recovered?'

'She is fully recovered, my Lord King.'

'Then why is she not here as she should be, to entertain her King?'

'She feels deep shame, your Majesty. Up until her rape, she had known only one man - you. She had always refused the advances of others because she valued your love and intended to keep herself pure and clean for you but, since her attack, she feels contaminated and unable to approach you.'

He looked thoughtful. 'I see. So you took it upon yourself to right this wrong?'

She bowed her head. 'I did, my Lord King.'

'Without my permission?'

'Yes, my Lord King.' She had failed her King and brought shame to the house of Achaemenia.

'And undermined the authority of the Commander of the Guard?'

'Yes, my Lord King.' Tears welled close to the surface as every eye in the room watched her.

Artabanus re-entered with Sataspes and stood before the King.

'Well,' said Khshayarsha to the culprit. 'What have you to say for yourself?'

Sataspes was clearly nervous despite his father's confidence. 'I did a serious wrong, your Majesty. I implore your forgiveness.'

'He is but a boy,' laughed the father of the young man. 'Your Queen has made a grave error in this matter.'

The King was furious. 'I will be the one to decide who has made grave errors, Artabanus.'

The room fell silent once more. The King stood up and faced Sataspes. 'For abusing a member of the royal household within the city limits, I hereby sentence you to...' He looked at Artabanus. 'Death by impalement.'

Sataspes bowed his head and Artabanus went as white as a sheet.

The King faced them. 'I will not have my authority undermined while I am away from the city. Let it be written in the laws of the Persians and Medes that, while I am absent, the Queen's word is my word. So let it be spoken and written to the length and breadth of the Empire.'

He turned to Sataspes once more. 'Because you have repented of your action and the Queen has intervened in your behalf, your sentence is hereby suspended conditionally.'

The young man raised his head with a quick sideways glance of thanks to Astur. 'What are the conditions, my Lord King? Speak and I will obey.'

'You are, I believe, a sailor of some prowess?'

'I am, your Majesty.'

'Very well. Tomorrow, you will march to the Nile with a chosen crew and will commandeer a suitable ship. From there, you will sail westward along the Lybian coast. I have heard that, beyond the pillars of Hercules, there is a wide ocean which borders the Land of Sands. You will follow this coast until you come to the land of Kush and then navigate the Nile Canal until you return to Egypt. Do this great act and your life is spared.'

The young man was ecstatic. 'It shall be done as you command.'

The King turned to the older man. 'Artabanus of the Achaemenids. For rebellion against my law and Queen I should have you banished to the Kavir. However, because of your past loyalty, I will waver the sentence and simply confirm your removal from the office of Commander of the Guard.'

Artabanus looked stunned and the King's sons were clearly unhappy that their unknown step-mother had just taken precedence over their great-uncle.

'Leave me,' said the King eventually.

A murmur ran through the guests as Artabanus left in shame and the King reclined once more.

The Queen leant close to the King and spoke in a whisper. 'But I did not intervene in behalf of Sataspes.'

'Ah. But you were going to, weren't you?'

'Yes, I was. But how did you know?'

'I am King,' he said with mock pomposity. 'I know everything.'

A MONTH expired before the news arrived which changed everything. The Greek General Themistocles who had saved the population of Athens by persuading them to withdraw and who had then led the Greek navy to defeat the Persian fleet at Salamis was discredited by extremists and subsequently forced into exile. Ever since the battle to take Athens, a kind of status quo had been observed in the occupied Greek territories. Mardonius, after a couple of unfruitful skirmishes south of the isthmus, had withdrawn to Asopus near Thebes for the winter. Themistocles, realising the futility of trying to raise an army large enough to push the Persians out of Macedonia, had thereby endeavoured to avoid further bloodshed by meeting secretly with Mardonius in order to form an alliance whereby the Greeks would be allowed to go about their normal daily lives and the Persian ego would be satisfied. It was in the middle of these fruitful arrangements which would keep both parties happy, that the fickle Athenians about-faced and declared Themistocles a traitor and gave command of the armed forces to recalled exiles Aristides and Xanthiapus.

It took all spring and summer for the Athenians to build up enough courage and manpower to challenge the Persians but, eventually, this they did in the northern foothills of Mount Cithaeron, close to Plataea. Mardonius, still hopeful of a chance to keep the peace and continue as Satrap, did not take the rebellion seriously. Instead of calling up Artabazanes in Thrace for assistance, he opted to go it alone and initially forced the army of one-hundred-and-ten thousand Greeks to retreat to the hills during the night. The Greek army was not much smaller than that of Persia and had Mardonius taken them seriously or sent a message to Artabazanes, the Persians would have held Greece for much longer than they did. Instead, the following morning, Mardonius followed the Greeks into the hills. The Spartan and Tegean Hoplites, under their commander, Pausanius, then used their own hills to their advantage and charged downhill at the double and overwhelmed the over-confident Persians. After but a few hours of fighting, Mardonius was killed and, without their leader, the totally demoralised Persians turned and fled in panic. On the same day, the Greek fleet changed to the offensive and King Leotychidas of Sparta launched his attack on the Persian fleet near Cape Mycale on the Asiatic coast close to Samos. The Persians beached their boats but Leotychidas landed to the north and, quite out of character for Greek seamen, marched overland and attacked from an entirely unexpected direction.

It was not a complete rout. Artabazanes, wisely realising something was very definitely afoot, marched on the Greeks and firmly prevented any further advance towards Bythinia. However, in little more than one day, the Persians had lost virtually all they had gained during the whole of the previous year. Hostilities were to continue for a further thirteen years but, at least for the time being, any hopes Khshayarsha had nurtured of a Persian Europe had been abruptly dashed to pieces.

The King took the news badly and went into severe depression. Astur and the now-reconciled Artaynte tried their best to bring him out of it but Khshayarsha turned in on himself and would hardly see or speak to anyone. Work continued at Persepolis, of course, but it had lost all sense of urgency without the drive from the King. If it hadn't been for the shrewd Haman, all control would have been lost. Visitors or emissaries were forbidden into the King's presence as he became almost paranoid about security. Everywhere he went, the Immortals accompanied him and simply to gain audience became a long and drawn-out process. Unless summoned, no-one was allowed into the royal presence and, without a specific invitation, any visitor to the palace was immediately executed without trial or reason. When in the King's company, a visitor was commanded to keep his hands inside his sleeves and any departure from this brought instant death from the guards whose instructions were very clear in the matter. Even the King's own sons were not exempt.

Crown Prince Darius was infuriated over the matter. 'This is ridiculous. How on earth can we carry on the government of a World Empire like this?'

'You worry too much, my brother,' replied the younger Artakhshayarsha. 'Father will get over it when he has done with sulking over his precious Greece.'

'Now go and wash your mouth out,' said Astur firmly. 'I will not have you mocking your father in this way. He has done as much as anyone to hold the Empire together and even your grandfather got no further than Marathon.'

'Ah, yes,' said Artakhshayarsha. 'But he didn't get all

depressed about it.'

'Maybe not. But your father has been under a lot of pressure lately. What he needs is help, not criticism.'

'Will that do any good?' asked Artaynte from her couch.

Astur lifted her arms in the air. 'I don't know, I really don't know. Even I have been banished from his presence.'

'I'm not surprised,' sneered Artakhshayarsha. 'Making a fool of him over that Sataspes affair.'

Astur simply glared at him.

'I think you had better apologise for that remark,' said Artaynte, swinging her feet to the floor.

Darius stepped between them. 'None of this is helping. I think, Artakhshayarsha, you had better keep a civil tongue in your head. Insulting the Queen will not improve anything.'

The younger son stood up. 'I might have known you would take her side in all this. You've had your beady eyes on our precious step-mother ever since we arrived from Persepolis. I suppose you want to bed her yourself now our father has lost interest in her.'

The sound of the slap echoed from the marble walls as Artaynte confronted the Prince with a face red with rage. Artakhshayarsha raised his hand to her.

'Stop!' said Astur. 'I will not have you striking my maid or any other woman in the palace.'

He glared at her. 'You would dare to threaten me, the son of the King?'

Astur walked slowly towards him and placed a long finger in the middle of his chest. 'You know the law of the Persians and Medes, Artakhshayarsha. No-one is exempt, not even you.'

The young man muttered some foul obscenity under his breath and then stomped out of the room.

'I'm sorry,' sighed Astur to Darius. 'That was unkind of me.'

'But truthful,' said the Crown Prince. 'Perhaps such truth should be heard more often in Shushan.'

Astur smiled. 'When you become King, my Lord Darius, make it your aim.'

'You know something? I might just do that.'

PRIME Minister Haman was not a happy man. Already upset about his own daughter not being chosen as Queen, he was now mortally offended. After passing the gateway on his way from the Palace, he met someone he knew. 'So, my Lord Artabanus, I see you are still in Shushan.'

'It is my home. I stay in case the King changes his mind as I am sure he will one day.'

Haman laughed as he strode away from the pathetic ex-Commander of the Guard. Then, he suddenly stopped and turned back to Artabanus. 'What if I could get you back into the King's favour?'

Artabanus looked surprised. 'How could you do that?'

'I alone have the ear of the King at the moment. I think he could be persuaded. By me, of course.'

'I would be grateful.'

Haman leered. 'How grateful?'

'Very grateful.'

'I thought as much. Tell me. The man at the gate over there. Who is he?'

Artabanus turned and looked. 'That is Marduka, officer of the gates.'

'He does not bow down to me when I pass. It is no great thing in itself but I am curious.'

'And you would like me to make enquiries?'

Haman smiled. 'I think you and I understand each other.'

ARTAYNTE walked quickly across the market place in the dusk of the evening. Knocking on the wooden door, she entered. Mordecai stood up. 'Artaynte, how good to see you.'

'And you, Marduka.'

'Do you have news of my Astur?'

'I do,' she said as she sat down. 'But first, I must inform you that she is worried about you.'

'Worried about me? Why on earth should she do that?'

'News has reached the palace that you are refusing to bow before the Prime Minister.'

'And so?'

'But why not? You always bowed before Lord Artabanus. Why do you refuse to bow before Haman?'

He sat down to face her. 'It is a long story.'

'You must tell me. You see, the King has specifically commanded that all bow down before the Prime Minister, whoever he may be.'

'And you think the King will enforce the law in my case?'

'It is the law. Khshayarsha will have no option if it is brought to his attention.'

He sighed. 'The matter goes back many years. Our ancestor was a man called Jacob who had a brother called Esau. Jacob grew up to be a man of God whilst Esau became a rebel.'

The Princess shrugged. 'Every family has its black sheep.'

'It is more serious than that, dearest Artaynte. Whereas Jacob's sons, the Jews, became a peace-loving people, Esau's descendants went out of their way to mistreat their relatives. For a time, the Jews went into slavery in Egypt but were eventually released.'

'How do you know all this?'

'We, too, have our law. Within it is the history of Moses.'

'Sorry, I didn't mean to stop you.'

'When the Jews were released from Egypt, they had to travel across the great desert of Zin. A branch of Esau's family lived there and, by rights, they should have assisted their kinfolk. Instead of that, they attacked them continually, cruelly killing the women and children because they were not courageous enough to take on the men. Because of their action our God, Jehovah, decreed in the law that, forever, these Amalekites were to be a cursed people.'

'But surely, after all these years, your God will have forgotten.'

'Not so. Many years after that, the Amalekites were still up to their old tricks and one of them, a king by the name of Agag, maliciously attacked the peaceful Jews and thereafter the Agagites were condemned to death forever.'

'And Haman is an Agagite?'

'Yes.'

'And you will not bow down to him for that reason?'

'Correct.'

'Not even a little bow to keep the King happy?'

'No.'

'For me?' she pleaded.

He looked down. 'I'm sorry, Artaynte.'

She placed her hand on his arm. 'Please. I don't want to lose you.'

'No.'

'Not for Astur?'

'Not even for Astur. I would die first.'

She gripped his hands tightly. 'I do believe Haman does have just that in mind for you.'

'Then so be it. I will not break the law of my God just as the King will not break his law.'

'I see. I will inform Astur. I only hope she will understand.'

ARTABANUS crept up to the house and was allowed entry by the guard. He was shown into a large room that seemed full of people.

'Artabanus,' called Haman across the room. 'Come in, come in. You have met my wife, Zeresh?'

Artabanus greeted a woman of obvious wealth and who knew it. 'I am delighted,' he said and was given wine by an attendant.

Eventually, Haman took him aside. 'What news, Artabanus?'

'It is concerning the little enquiry I was to make for you.'

'Yes?'

'It is nothing of consequence; some feudal matter from centuries ago. Apparently, this Marduka's real name is Mordecai and he is a Jew.'

The whole room suddenly fell silent as Haman stared at him and then slowly put down his cup of wine. 'You are sure of this?'

'I have it on good authority, My Lord. Is it important?'

Haman smiled wickedly. 'It is now.' He walked around for a moment in the stark silence and then faced Artabanus. 'You have done well. I shall inform the King of your good work in this matter.'

Still not seeing the significance, Artabanus simply smiled and nodded as the murmur of conversations broke out around the room.

'You must use him as an example,' said a younger man.

Haman nodded thoughtfully. 'Perhaps, Dalphon.'

'Just inform the King. He will have him executed.'

'It may be,' said Zeresh slyly. 'That there is a better way.'

'Yes, my love?'

'I understand that, in his present mood, the King will sign anything you recommend to him. Is that not so, my husband?'

Haman nodded. 'Within reason.'

'And if you suggested the death of a mere gatekeeper, he would agree to it?'

'Without giving it a thought.'

'Suppose,' she said. 'Just suppose that you also proposed the death of his family.'

'I am sure such an eventuality would be implied automatically. It is traditional that a man's family can be executed along with the lawbreaker himself.'

'All his family?'

'Usually.'

'I mean... ALL his family, regardless of where they live?'

Haman stopped suddenly and grinned. 'I knew there had to be a good reason for marrying you all those years ago.'

'You get my meaning?'

'I do.' He stroked his beard as he paced. 'Maybe I could get the King to sign the decree without being specific as to numbers.'

'You realise what this could mean?'

'Yes. Hundreds of them, dying.'

'Thousands of them,' corrected Zeresh.

Dalphon interjected. 'Perhaps even millions.'

'Yes. And there is no law that says the decree is limited to Shushan or even Persia. Just think of it.' He rubbed his hands in glee. 'Every Jew, dead. Every single one of them.'

'And we will not have had to do a thing. We just sit back and watch it happen.'

'And listen to their screams,' said Dalphon. 'Oh, how I remember that young Jewish woman we used on the road from Babylon. Do you remember, Poratha?'

'Do I indeed? All those lovely screams that echoed around the hills.'

'Music to my ears,' said Aridatha.
'What about the girl?' asked Poratha.
'Girl?' asked their father suddenly.
'They had a child of about twelve or so.'
'What happened to her?'
'She ran away.'
'Ran away?' Zeresh asked with sudden concern. 'Did you catch her?'
'No. We lost her in the dark.'
Zeresh clutched her son's arm tightly. 'If she can identify any of you, you know what that will mean, don't you?'
'Relax, mother. She fell into the river and went over the falls. I expect there are little pieces of her all the way to the sea.'
Zeresh relaxed noticeably. 'You had me worried for a moment.'
'Don't be. Soon all the other Jews will follow her fate.'
'I drink to that day. Jewish men and women dying all over the Empire.'
'And their sons?'
'They must all go, too.'
'Even the young girls?' asked Arisai with sadistic enthusiasm.
Haman sneered. 'We don't want them having little Jewish babies, do we? We must disembowel every one.'
'When?' asked Zeresh with undisguised glee.
'I will consult Zoroaster,' said Haman.
'Can you do it?'
'Of course. Am I not known as Memucan, chief of the Magi, gifted with the sight of the gods?'
'When?' asked Dalphon eagerly as his father cast lots.
'It is the twelfth month,' Haman declared after consideration.
'But that is almost a year from now,' despaired Zeresh.
'Patience, my dear,' said Haman. 'It will be worth it to see

their dead bodies everywhere. If fact, it will be worth it just to see Marduka die for his insolence.'

'What is the day, father?'

Haman consulted the oracle. 'The thirteenth day.'

'We have a date,' said Zeresh. 'We must use it well.'

'We must first get the matter past the King,' cautioned Haman.

'Just give him the document to sign, he will do it for you.'

'Yes, but he is not stupid. If he even half suspects that some of them may be loyal subjects, he will have my head instead.'

'Then don't tell him,' suggested Zeresh. 'Simply put it to him that they are rebels, traitors who intend to rise up and overthrow his Empire. You don't have to be specific about who or how many there are.'

'If he knew how many, he would certainly ask questions. The document must be worded very carefully.'

'Perhaps,' interrupted Artabanus with a slight cough. 'Perhaps I could assist in that matter. With my past experience, I could formulate such a document for you.'

Haman looked astonished. 'You would help us?'

'On one condition.'

'Yes?' said the wary Magi.

'When the deed is done, there will be outcry. The Jews have been well treated in the past by both Cyrus and Darius. They are known as a peace-loving people who have always paid their taxes and honoured the King.'

'Yes, I know that. But how will that help you?'

'Very much. You see, if they are annihilated in the way you have specified, many will rise up against Khshayarsha, especially if the event is accompanied by certain...propaganda.'

'And then what?'

'When the King is overthrown, as he almost certainly will be,

I want the throne.'

Haman said nothing for a moment. 'What if I wish the throne for myself?'

'Lord Haman. I am sure that you are well qualified in many respects but, unfortunately, you are not Persian and, more to the point, not of the Achaemenid dynasty, so the other Princes will not follow you and could even rebel against you. If, on the other hand, I was to rule, it would be acceptable.' He leant closer. 'We could always share the rulership when all the hue and cry has died down.'

Haman smiled. 'Artabanus, you may just have something there.'

'I know I have. You see, I also have another desire.'

'Which is?'

'I want to see the Queen die. I want her blood running down my spear, to hear her screams in my ears as I twist the blade inside her belly.'

Haman shook his head slowly. 'You must really hate her.'

'Yes. I hate her very much after the way she has humiliated me.'

'You will have almost a year to wait,' reminded Zeresh. 'The gods have spoken.'

'I can wait,' said Artabanus. 'If you can bear the sight of Marduka for that period, I can spend my time dreaming of the death of the Queen. From now on, every time I see her, I will think of the day which has been decided and that thought alone will give me considerable pleasure.'

A cool breeze wafted around the city as Prime Minister Haman was carried on his carriage through the gateway and into the palace at Shushan. In his hand was a document prepared with the consultation of Artabanus and, as he passed through the gateway, everyone bowed except Marduka who simply stood in the shadow of the doorway as he passed. Never mind, smiled Haman to himself, don't get yourself upset. It will all be over sooner than you think. If you just knew what I had in my hand, Marduka, you would fall at my feet like a slave and beg for my mercy. Still, it is too late now. In a matter of hours, the decree will be issued; provided, of course, I can get the matter past the King.

Khshayarsha sat on the throne as the Magi approached and was stopped by the guards. The King held out his golden sceptre as usual and Haman was admitted to the royal presence.

'Are you well, my Lord King?'

'What news?' asked the King, ignoring Haman's pleasantries.

'Good news and bad news, my Lord King. Your elder brother, Artabazanes, has returned from Thrace with news of a minor advance. I recommend that you appoint him Satrap of Dascylium and Cilicia for his bravery.'

The King waved his arm vaguely. 'You deal with the matter. It is of little consequence to me. Anything else?'

'Yes. Sataspes has sent word that he has reached the south of the Land of Sands and has discovered little black men who cover themselves only in palm leaves.'

'When is he expected back?'

'Not for many months, my Lord King.'

'Anything else?' He was getting impatient.

'Unfortunately, yes, Sire. There is news of a minor rebellion in the Empire. A people with a hatred for the laws of the King has risen up against you and are at present raising an army to overthrow your Empire.'

Khshayarsha turned. 'Who would dare do such a thing?

Egypt? Babylon?'

'No, your Majesty. These people have deliberately scattered themselves throughout the whole of your Empire with a view to dividing it amongst themselves. They are but a small people of no great significance but they have planned to overthrow your power and assassinate you on the fourteenth day of the twelfth month.'

Khshayarsha slammed his fist on the arm of his throne. 'They must be annihilated.'

'My sentiments precisely. I would, however, recommend delaying our attack upon them for a while so as to make sure we have all of them in our hands and none escape. I suggest you send out instructions to all the Satraps of the Empire to destroy this miserable people on the previous day when they will have gathered themselves together.'

'The idea does seem a sound one, Haman. But will it not cost a large amount of silver and gold?'

'It is true, my Lord King. However, to show the extent of my deep loyalty to you, I will pay for this deed out of my own treasure chest.'

The King raised his eyebrows at the gesture. 'Indeed?'

Haman tried to hide his sneer. 'It is the very least I could do for my great King.'

'Very well,' said Khshayarsha with a dismissive gesture. 'Arrange it for me.'

'I have already made out the document of judgement for you to authorise.' Haman held his breath while he offered it to the King.

'Don't bother me now. We have plenty of time.'

'With respect, highness. Our Satraps will need to be ready so they can closely observe the guilty ones.'

The King thought for a moment and then removed his seal-ring.

'Here, you deal with the matter in my name. Send out the proclamation if you feel it is right. Seal my name and all will obey.'

Haman looked at the gold seal-ring in his hand and thought of the possibilities it offered. Perhaps Artabanus had been right. Not only was the destruction of the Jews now within his grasp, but rulership as well.

He bowed. 'It shall be done as you command.'

HAMAN watched as the King's secretaries copied the document and made translations into the many languages needed; Greek, Aramaic, Sanskrit, Egyptian Hieroglyphic, Sumerian Cuneiform and many others. By post, copies were sent to the most distant parts of the Empire as well as being nailed up in and around Shushan. Haman took particularly sadistic delight in sending Marduka his own, personal copy. As the peace of the city was disturbed by a mixture of anger and mourning, Khshayarsha drank wine with Haman, blissfully unaware of just what had been done by his Prime Minister.

At the same time, Artaynte rushed into Astur's presence, frantic with worry. 'Astur, it is Marduka. He has gone into mourning.'

Astur sat up suddenly. 'Why would he do that? Who has died?'

'I had a job getting anything coherent out of him but he muttered something about a proclamation which has been issued by the King.'

Astur's face went dark. 'Proclamation? What proclamation?'

'I don't know, Astur. I wasn't able to find out.'

The Queen stood up and clapped her hands. 'Hathach. Go with Artaynte and see if you can find out what it is that has caused so much unhappiness to Marduka.'

'Very well, your Majesty.'

'And take fresh clothes for him. By tradition, he will have ripped his own clothes in mourning.'

He bowed. 'I will go at once.'

'And report back to me personally,' she instructed, wagging her finger. 'Personally, do you understand?'

The Royal Eunuch nodded. 'It shall be done as you so command, my Queen.'

HATHACH and Artaynte found Mordecai in the outer courtyard and offered him the clean garments Astur had supplied.

'I cannot wear them, my child,' he replied in anguish. 'Our mourning is very great indeed.'

'But what has happened?' asked Hathach with concern. 'The Queen is most distressed at your condition.'

'It is the proclamation from the King.' He reached into the folds of his garment and produced his copy of the document.

Artaynte read it and then read it again and slowly sat down. 'It does not mention the Jews by name.'

'Perhaps not. But it is certainly implied. What other people worship the god called Jehovah? Who else go up to Jerusalem to worship? Throughout the whole of the world, there will be no-one who will be in any doubt as to who is meant. A great many peoples will love this opportunity to get rid of us.'

'But not everyone hates the Jews, surely.'

'Perhaps not. Nevertheless, even those who do not actually hate us are envious of the prosperity of many of our people.'

Artaynte consulted the document once more. 'And the proclamation quite clearly states that any person killing these people may gain possession of their lands and property as spoil.'

'Precisely. Many who would normally not raise a hand against us will be tempted by the offer of great wealth.'

'Whoever it was who issued this carefully-worded decree was very clever indeed.'

'There is no doubt as to who wrote it. It is the work of Haman the Magi.'

'I know you said his family has a traditional feud with the Jews but I can't believe that even our Prime Minister would go to these lengths to vent his hatred.'

'You don't know him,' interrupted Hathach. 'I knew him before he came to Shushan. He can be very vindictive when he wants to be.'

Artaynte was deep in thought. 'I know Astur does not like him though I've never quite understood why.'

'Astur is in a very difficult position. She knows of the hatred between the Jews and the Agagites but, fortunately for her, she has never been in a position of having to bow down to him. As Queen, she can remain aloof from it all.'

'Astur is not uncaring,' protested Artaynte.

'I didn't intend to suggest she was. I merely meant that my problem has not yet become hers.'

Artaynte clutched at her heart. 'You mean...?'

'Exactly. How long do you think it will be before Haman puts two and two together? Eventually, someone is bound to find out that our little Hadasseh, too, is a Jew.'

'But how? We have said nothing.'

Marduka sighed. 'People like Haman and Artabanus will make it their job to find out. With the hatred Artabanus has for Astur, I wouldn't put it past him to personally want to carry out the sentence. He hates her for making a fuss over the fact that Sataspes raped you and blames Astur for everything which has happened to him ever since.'

Artaynte jumped to her feet. 'Then we must find a way to put a stop to it.'

'How can we do that? Haman was very clever in getting Khshayarsha to agree to it. The Satraps and Princes will carry out the King's word to the letter.'

'Do you suppose the King knows what has happened?'

'I have no idea. I cannot bring myself to believe he would have agreed to the proclamation if he knew that Astur was a Jew.'

'Do you think Haman already knows?'

'I wouldn't put it past him,' said the Queen's eunuch. 'With Astur out of the way, he will feel he has total control of the King.'

'If the King finds out, will he stop the proclamation?'

'He cannot. It is a law of the Persians and Medes which cannot be changed or altered in any way.'

Artaynte paced the room and wrung her hands in desperation. 'Then what can be done?'

'Someone must ensure that the King is aware of what has happened. He is a just man and he will know what to do.'

'It is impossible. Only Haman is allowed to see the King.'

Mordecai sighed. 'And I cannot see Haman imploring salvation for the Jews.'

'You are right. However, I will make sure that Astur knows what is happening. May I keep this copy of the decree to show her?'

'Of course, my child.' Mordecai smiled. 'Though I know not what good it will do. If Astur cannot go to see the King, then all is lost.'

ASTUR read the decree in silence and then got to her feet and stared out of the palace window for a long time. The mountains seemed to shimmer in the noon-day heat and took on a purplish tinge. Beneath them, the desert road looked barren and yellow.

'What does Mordecai suggest I do?'

'He says you must speak to the King.'

She bowed her head as the tears came to her eyes. 'How can I do that? He has not even asked to see me for a month.'

'And,' added Hathach, 'Anyone who tries to see the King uninvited is instantly executed, whoever they are.'

Artaynte moved closer. 'Mordecai did make the point that your own life is in danger, even if you do nothing.'

Astur whirled on her friend, tears of frustration welling just below the surface. 'Do you really think I care what happens to me? I would willingly die for my people. In fact, I would risk execution simply to save Mordecai if I thought it would do any good. But how can I just throw away my life for nothing?'

Hathach coughed nervously. 'With respect, highness. If you are known to be a Jew, you may have little choice in the matter. You will be killed yourself. Even the King will not be able to break his own law.'

'Yes,' agreed Artaynte. 'Remember the story you told me about your relative Daniel? King Darius was tricked into issuing a similar proclamation in Babylon and Daniel himself was sentenced to death in the Lions' den. According to your Holy Book, the great Darius was unable to prevent the sentence being carried out even when he found out that it was his closest advisor who was to suffer. Fortunately for Daniel, it worked out all right. But the point stands, if Mordecai dies, you die.'

'I am not afraid to die,' said Astur sadly.

'I know you are not and neither is Mordecai. He is simply

concerned for all the other thousands of innocent men, women and children.' She paused. 'He also said something else.'

'Yes?'

Artaynte took a deep breath. 'He said it is possible that your God has chosen you as Queen for Khshayarsha with just this eventuality in mind.'

Astur looked at her friend for a long time and then held her head high. 'In that case, I must do it. I will go before the King.'

'Perhaps he will not execute his little Hadasseh,' said Artaynte quietly.

'Perhaps not,' said the Queen. 'Hathach!'

The eunuch bowed. 'Yes, your Majesty.'

'Go to Marduka and beg him to entreat the people to fast and pray in my behalf. I shall do the same. In three days, I have heard, Haman will be away from the city until midday and I shall seize the opportunity to attempt to see the King in this matter.'

'Your highness,' said the eunuch. 'It is not just the Jews who will pray for you. We will all do so.'

The Queen touched his face gently. 'You are a good man, Hathach.'

'Just remember, my Queen. So is the King, deep at heart.'

Astur smiled. 'I hope, for all our sakes, that you are right.'

ASTUR rose with the sun and waited as Artaynte did her black hair in the way that she knew Khshayarsha liked it, long with curls down the sides, like a child's. When she had finished, the royal headdress of finely-spun silk was placed on top. Discarding many of the usual fineries, Astur opted for the thin, summer apparel of the Queens of Persia - white cotton with red sash and hem.

'You look great,' said Artaynte with feeling. 'If the King does not agree to see you now, he must be out of his tiny mind.'

'That,' said Astur quietly, 'Is precisely what the problem may be.'

'Whoops! I didn't use a very good choice of words there, did I?'

'You spoke from the heart, as always.' Astur smiled and turned to Hathach. 'Is everything ready?'

He bowed. 'It is as you commanded, your Majesty.'

'Thank you. You may go now.'

Hathach left. Astur reached out and touched her maid's cheek. 'This might well be goodbye, my dear friend.'

Artaynte raised her head high. 'This is not the end, it is the beginning. Go and seduce the King before I do it for you.'

They both laughed together for a moment before Astur turned without another word and stepped, barefoot, from the house of the women.

KHSHAYARSHA sat on his throne surrounded by guards as he signed various documents presented to him by Harbona. A slight commotion made him look up.

'What is the matter with you men?' he growled.

One or two of them looked at each other and then glanced towards the far doorway.

'It is the Queen in the courtyard,' one whispered.

'What will the King do?'

'She is very brave to come uninvited with the King in the mood he has been in lately.'

'Will he have her executed?'

The King smiled and Astur stepped forward. One of the

guards raised his sword to protect the King.

'Spare her,' the King commanded and held out the royal sceptre to her as a sign of recognition and acceptance.

The Queen stepped close and touched the tip of the sceptre as a gesture of submission to the King and Khshayarsha turned to Harbona who was clearly more than a little relieved at the apparent reconciliation.

'Leave me.'

Harbona hesitated until Khshayarsha looked at his guards and said, 'All of you. Go!'

Still uncertain as to whether they had him heard him right, all but two attendants departed.

Khshayarsha smiled. 'You look very pleasing, my Queen. How can I reward you this fine day?'

Astur swallowed. 'I have but a small request, my Lord King.'

'Name it, up to half my Kingdom.'

'I do not desire riches, my Lord King. I simply desire the presence of my husband and his Prime Minister at a great banquet this evening.'

'A banquet? For me?'

'For who else, my Lord King?'

'I am honoured.' The King turned to his attendant. 'See that Haman is informed the minute he arrives. He is to attend the banquet of the Queen.'

'With respect, your Majesty. He will be tired after his long ride.'

'Tired or not. Ensure he is there at my command.'

The attendant bowed. 'It shall be as you desire, O mighty one.'

The King turned to Astur. 'You really are looking remarkably radiant this morning.'

Astur smiled. 'I must say you are obviously feeling better in yourself.'

He leant forward. 'I have good news.'

Astur looked puzzled as she took the seat offered to her. 'Good news, my Lord King?'

He handed her a scroll which she opened. It was written in a foreign tongue. 'It is from Themistocles.'

'The Greek Admiral?'

'Greek Ex-Admiral. For the last couple of years he has been exiled in Argos. He has written to me secretly and says he now wants to come to Persia and show me a way that we can defeat the Greek army and navy. If anyone can help me to regain my pride, it is he.'

'That is indeed good news,' Astur agreed to keep him happy. Anything which kept a smile on the King's face right now had to be good news. 'Then my banquet will be welcome.'

'You couldn't have timed it better, my dear. Tonight, there will be much merrymaking.'

Astur sighed with relief. Tonight, at the banquet, she would expose Haman for what he was.

THE arrangements went according to plan. Khshayarsha arrived as the food was served and Haman, looking tired, a short time after. The wine flowed freely and Astur desperately wanted to find the right moment to speak but it eluded her. The King was so engrossed in his news that it was very late by the time that he got close enough to speak with her.

'This is the greatest banquet of all time, Astur,' said the King with glazed eyes. 'You have excelled yourself.'

'You have indeed, my Queen,' agreed the Prime Minister.

'I am glad I have pleased you, my Lords.'

'It is a great honour,' said Haman. 'To be entertained by the

Queen of the Persians. I am flattered to have been invited.'

Astur desperately wanted to broach the subject closest to her heart but the King was obviously the worse for drink and Haman was being so nice that she chickened out. Instead, she said, 'The evening is not yet over. I have a very special treat for my husband.'

'Special treat? For me?' He leaned closer. 'But first you must tell me what I can do for you. What is your greatest wish? Name it and it is yours, up to half my Kingdom.'

'I wish...' She paused. 'For now, I simply wish that you would come to a further banquet I have arranged for tomorrow. It is then that I shall reveal my greatest desire.'

'So be it. If it is anything like tonight, it will be worth it.'

'You must both come,' insisted Astur. 'And the Crown Princes, Darius and Artakhshayarsha.'

'I have sent Artakhshayarsha to Persepolis. If Themistocles is coming to Persia, he must see my new palace in its finished state. My son will put pressure upon the builders to ensure it is completed in time for his visit next year.'

'It is a good plan,' agreed the Queen and then stood up. 'Now, my Lord King. If you are ready, I present to you the highlight of the evening. I offer you - the Golden Princess.'

The room fell silent as the oil lamps were dimmed and the drums started to beat out a steady rhythm. Astur sat behind the King, her hands holding his head tenderly against her breast as the stringed instruments started to play a haunting tune. As the notes reached a crescendo, the far curtains parted and six maidens swept in and began to dance in front of them. The eyes of Khshayarsha and Haman flicked from one to the other of the dancers as they gyrated and swung their heads around in dizzy circles and their hair fanned out. When all was at a climax, a seventh dancer appeared, dressed from head to toe in golden silk. Her veil was high and her eyes dark as she weaved in and out of the other girls, swinging her body around in time with the music. Astur watched as the King smacked his lips in anticipation. Barefoot, the Golden Princess leapt around until, with a flourish, she cast off both veil and headdress.

'It is Artaynte,' breathed the King.

'The Golden Princess is my present to you for tonight,' said Astur quietly.

'It is accepted with grateful thanks, my Queen. Tomorrow, I shall repay you with her weight in gold.'

'Only if she pleases you, my Lord King.'

'She will, I know.'

'Then take her, my Lord King. Go now, while the mood is right. Spend the night in ecstasy with your favourite concubine and dream only of love.'

The King smiled his thanks. 'It will be your turn tomorrow.'

Astur nodded as the King rose to his feet and held out his hands to the laughing Artaynte.

'Yes,' Astur said under her breath as she swallowed nervously. 'My turn tomorrow. But my turn for what?'

HAMAN staggered from the banquet into the darkness of the palace garden. In spite of the lateness of the hour, it was still oppressively hot. Soon, summer would be near and anyone with any sense would move to Ecbatana until Autumn. His heart was merry as his attendants helped him towards the gateway leading to his house. A movement beside the gateway made him smile.

'Good day, Marduka,' he called mockingly. 'Aren't you going to bow before your superior?'

'With respect, you are drunk, Haman, and bring shame upon

the household of the King.'

Haman laughed. 'Drunk, am I? At least I am alive which is more than you will be soon.'

'I rest my faith in my Lord Jehovah. If it is his will that I die, then I die. If he wants me to live, he will find a way to save our people.'

'Don't bank on it,' said Haman, becoming angry.

The servants intervened. 'It is late, my Lord. It is best that we get you home quickly.'

Haman sighed. 'So be it. I can wait.' He stared at Marduka and then grinned. 'I can wait.'

His attendants helped him through the gateway and down the road until they reached his home where his wife awaited him.

'Where have you been?' Zeresh demanded to know. 'It is late.'

'Silence, wife. Call my sons to me.'

'But most of them are in bed. I cannot wake them at this hour.'

'You must. I have something to tell them.'

'Very well.' She left as Haman sat down and drank more wine until they had assembled before him along with their wives and the many friends who were staying in his large mansion.

'I have been deeply honoured today. I have been to a banquet with the King and Queen.'

'The Queen?' asked the surprised Dalphon. 'I thought she and the King were not on speaking terms.'

'They are now,' he said conspiratorially. 'And what is more, the Queen has specifically invited me to a further banquet tomorrow afternoon.'

'That is indeed a great honour,' said Zeresh. 'It is rare that someone is invited to the palace by the Queen. Unheard of twice in two days. They must value your services highly.'

'That's what I thought,' he replied smugly. 'In fact, if it wasn't for that Marduka in the gate, everything would be just fine.'

'Does he still not bow to you, father?' asked Poratha.

'He does not. He stands and mocks me with his eyes. I can see it clearly.'

'Even in the dark?' asked Zeresh with a laugh.

'Even in the dark. I don't know how much longer I can endure such humiliation. One the one hand, I am honoured far above my expectations and, on the other, humiliated by a mere Jew.'

'Then deal with the matter yourself? He has broken the King's law, has he not?'

Haman nodded. 'He has indeed.'

'Then why not make an example of him. I am sure the King will give you permission to have him executed. After all, he is nothing to the King. Khshayarsha will probably never give the matter a second thought if you were to ask. He will not want to get involved with a simple lawbreaker.'

'You are right, my wife. I will do it in the morning.'

'There is something else you can do, father,' added Dalphon. 'Why not have him hung up so that all the other Jews will see his body and it will help them to imagine what they have coming to them in a few months' time?'

Haman grinned. 'You are indeed my own son, Dalphon. A gallows it shall be.'

'A high one so all may see.'

'Ten cubits high so he can be seen from anywhere in the market place.'

'If you make it twenty, all in the lower city will see his body.'

Zeresh smiled. 'If you are going to do this, why not do it properly? How high will it have to be so that all in Shushan will see his body rotting in the sun?'

'It would have to be very high,' Dalphon calculated. 'Probably forty or fifty cubits.'

'Then fifty it shall be. My sons, first thing in the morning you must make a start on these gallows. I shall get the King to sign the death warrant tomorrow and, by the time I come out from the banquet in the evening, I shall be able to see his body hanging on the rope. I shall sleep all the better for it.'

ARTAYNTE stirred restlessly in the King's chamber. Although it was not yet summer, even the nights at Shushan were already overbearingly hot and humid. She peered towards the window where the faint breeze moved the curtain slightly.

A hand touched her arm. 'Can you not sleep either?'

'No, my Lord King. It is so dreadfully hot.' She slipped her feet to the floor and stepped to the arched window overlooking the courtyard. Guards moved in the shadows as they closely watched all entrances to the palace. There was to be no repetition of the last incident.

'It was a dream which woke me,' said the King as he joined her at the window and stared up at the stars which twinkled brightly against a backdrop of inky blackness.

Artaynte turned to face him. 'A dream, my Lord King?'

He nodded. 'One which has left me more than a little unsettled. In it, a god who must have been Ahura-Mazda appeared to me and chastised me for disobeying the law.'

'You have never broken your law. You uphold the laws of the Persians and Medes to the letter as did your father.'

'So I have always thought,' he said sadly. 'I have not always succeeded but I have tried to be a good king who was fair to everyone.'

'I can think of no way you could have made Ahura-Mazda angry.'

'He did not seem angry,' said Khshayarsha. 'Merely... disappointed in me. As if I had missed something important.'

'Why not ask Haman in the morning?'

'That is a good idea. Unless...'

'Yes?'

'Put something on,' he suddenly said and threw his own gown around his shoulders. He opened the inner door. 'Harbona.'

The attendant arrived quickly, sleep still in his eyes but his sword in his hand to defend his King.

Khshayarsha smiled. 'Put your weapon away, Harbona. I merely wish for you to fetch me the record book of the law.'

The attendant looked startled. 'The record book, your Majesty? At this time of night? Is there some discrepancy?'

'I hope not. I just wish to satisfy myself that all is well.'

Harbona bowed. 'As you command.' He left and, a few minutes later, returned with a large collection of scrolls which he placed before the King.

'You may go,' said Khshayarsha and he was alone again with the Queen's Maid of Honour. 'Now, where do I start?'

'Can I help?' asked Artaynte. 'Perhaps if I read out the pertinent parts, you could stop me if something doesn't make sense.'

Khshayarsha smiled. 'Very well.'

Artaynte selected a scroll at the King's instructions and began to read aloud as Khshayarsha paced, deep in thought.

'First there is the matter of the tribute from Ethiopia. The Satrap sends you five hundred camels and a thousand bushels of dates.'

Artaynte looked up at him but he shook his head.

'The next entry is for the week when Astur was chosen as Queen. It lists the concubines who were presented to you as well as your final choice. Then there are details of the banquet you ordered. Seven hundred gallons of milk, three hundred and twenty jars of the best wine...'

'No. Not that,' he said, waving his hand. 'Continue.'

'Then, there is Harbona's full report of the assassination attempt and Hegai's death whilst saving your life.'

'He was a good man,' said the King sadly.

'He was indeed, your Majesty.'

'Tell me,' said Khshayarsha suddenly. 'Does Harbona say who was responsible?'

'He lists Bigthana and Teresh, the two who were caught.'

'No. I mean, who was responsible for alerting the household. I know that you arrived and informed me personally, but who told you?'

'It was one of the royal gatekeepers, my Lord King.' Her heart quickened. 'It was Marduka.'

'Do I know this Marduka?'

'He is in the gate from the city. Apparently, he overheard the men plotting in the gateway and hastened to warn the palace. When no guards could be found, he called for me and I brought the message directly to yourself.'

'This Marduka. How has he been rewarded for his great loyalty?'

Artaynte bowed her head. 'He has not, my Lord King. Marduka did not do this thing for reward but because he has deep respect for his King.'

'He must be rewarded,' said Khshayarsha firmly. He pondered for a moment. 'Haman will tell me in the morning.

He will know the correct procedure for honouring such bravery and loyalty.'

HAMAN smiled as he left his home that next morning. Already, the sounds of hammering told him that his sons had started to build the gallows designed for Marduka. He got down from his carriage as he reached the palace and stepped towards the place where his King waited. Marduka's death warrant had already been written out and was in his hand as he strode into the courtyard. In a few minutes, the deed would be done and, by the time the day was out, Marduka would be dead. The first of a great many Jews to die.

'Ah, Haman,' greeted Khshayarsha as the Prime Minister entered before the throne. He placed his arm around his Prime Minister's shoulders. 'Tell me. What does the law say I must do with someone who pleases me very much? Someone to whom I wish to bring great honour?'

'Well,' said Haman thoughtfully, thinking there was surely no-one in the kingdom more worthy of honour than himself. 'It would vary according to the greatness of the deed. If this someone had served you well, it would be appropriate to give him the very highest honour.'

'And that is, my good friend?'

Good friend? He must be talking about me. 'If I was the King I would take this individual and clothe him with your own royal cloak of dignity and put upon his head a crown of pure gold.'

'And then?'

'And then I would seat him upon your own favourite stallion and have him paraded through the public square of the city of Shushan with one of your highest-ranking Princes to make announcement before him to all the people saying; "this is what happens to anyone who pleases the King. This is how he shall be treated." Then I would have his name proclaimed to the length and breadth of your great Empire.'

'That is what the law says?'

'It is, my Lord King,' said Haman smugly, Marduka's death warrant already in his sweaty little hand.

'You have spoken well and the honour is appropriate in this case. Go, do exactly as you have spoken. Take the man, Marduka, who is sitting in the palace gatehouse and clothe him with my own ceremonial crown and apparel. Sit him upon my own, personal stallion and go yourself and say the things you have spoken. Make sure that all are aware I have approved of this man.'

Haman gaped and found he could not move. Beneath his gown, his knees trembled and his hand tightly clutched the parchment in his hand.

'Did you have a matter to discuss with me first?' asked the King, frowning at the unread document.

Haman quickly pushed the damning scroll into his sleeve. 'It will wait. I will first carry out the command of my King.' He left hurriedly and Khshayarsha stared after him.

'Harbona,' said the King thoughtfully. 'Take a squad of the Immortals. I fear Haman looks a little worried about the assignment I have just given him. Ensure he remains unmolested at all times and is able to carry out fully all that I have commanded.'

'I shall see to the matter personally,' bowed the attendant who had clearly seen the implication of the matter.

MORDECAI looked up as Haman entered the gatehouse. Slowly, he lay down his scroll and got to his feet. He had not missed the significance of the gallows which were almost completed near the public square and guessed they were for him. He would like to have been given the opportunity to plead his case before the King but even that had obviously been denied him. He was sad his little Hadasseh was not there to see him die, probably not even being aware of the matter.

'I have come for you,' said the Prime Minister.

Mordecai nodded and, for the first time, noticed the palace guards Haman had brought with him. 'I am ready.'

Haman stepped aside as the gatekeeper came out into the bright sunshine and saw the King's personal attendant. Harbona nodded to Haman who took the royal cloak of deep purple and laid it around Mordecai's shoulders. Mordecai did not move as he stood, amazed, as the royal headdress was placed upon his head. As if in a dream, he was led to the great white stallion and helped up onto its back.

'This is what happens to anyone who pleases the King,' said Haman quietly. 'This is how he shall be treated.'

'Louder,' prompted Harbona who didn't particularly like the Prime Minister and was loving every moment of the drama.

Haman cleared his throat. 'This is what happens to anyone who pleases the King. This is how he shall be treated.'

With guard in tow, he led the horse through the gateway and into the public square. A crowd soon gathered.

'This is what happens to anyone who pleases the King,' Haman said again, realising he had lost his battle for the time being and had better keep the King happy or else he might find himself hung upon his own gallows. 'This is how he shall be treated.'

Harbona smiled as he followed the procession around and

people cheered and waved at the honour which had been granted to someone so highly respected in the community.

'This is what happens to anyone who pleases the King. This is how he shall be treated,' Haman called again and again as they passed the palace.

ZERESH greeted her husband as he entered, looking thoroughly miserable. 'Is it done?'

'Stupid woman. Have you not heard?' Haman asked angrily. 'It seems the whole of the rest of Elam has.'

His wife stood up. 'Heard what?'

He told her. She sat down slowly, her eyes glazed. 'We are finished.'

'There is still the decree. The law cannot be changed. If we can but last out the next few months, we shall still see all the Jews die.'

'Unless Marduka deals with us first.'

'He cannot. I am still Prime Minister and have jurisdiction over him. I may have failed this attempt but he will still die on the date chosen by the lot of the gods. Alternatively, we may have to find a less public way of getting rid of him.'

'I am sure you will think of something,' said Zeresh with a smile.

A servant entered. 'The King's attendant is here, my Lord.'

'The banquet,' said Haman suddenly. 'By Molech, I had forgotten.'

'Go to the banquet, my husband,' said Zeresh. 'Relax and forget your troubles. You can push all thoughts from your mind as you dine with the Queen.'

'Yes,' he said thoughtfully. 'The Queen of the Persians.'

THE King smiled when he saw the extent of the banquet

Astur had prepared. As the guests started to arrive, he sat upon his couch as she greeted them. Darius arrived soon and the Queen bowed low before him.

'I should bow to you, Astur,' he whispered.

'You are Crown Prince, Darius,' said Astur. 'I am merely Queen.'

'There is nothing "merely" about you, Astur. I admit that, like Artakhshayarsha, I was suspicious of you at first. I felt that no-one could replace our mother as Queen. However, I am happy to say we have been proved wrong. My father and I love you dearly.'

'And Artakhshayarsha?'

Darius laughed. 'Even my younger brother will come around one of these days. You have that kind of effect on people.'

'I do hope so, Darius. It upsets me when there is discord in the King's household.'

He kissed Astur's cheek tenderly and led her to her couch where she reclined beside the King. 'Don't let Artakhshayarsha get to you. You are all right.'

She smiled.

The King leaned close. 'This is remarkable, my dear. Even better than yesterday.'

'I am glad it pleases my Lord and King.'

'It does indeed. How can I repay you? I insist that you speak this time. Up to half of my kingdom if you will but ask.'

Astur took a deep breath. 'What I ask is not of great value to the Empire, Khshayarsha,' she replied quietly but confidently. 'Though of considerable value to me.'

The King frowned. 'Name it.'

She looked straight at him. 'You know who I am?'

'Of course. You are Astur, Queen of the Persians.'

'No,' she said. 'Who I really am?'

'You are my little Hadasseh, child of the river.'

'I am a Jew,' she said suddenly.

Khshayarsha smiled. 'I know that.'

Astur was taken-aback. 'You do?'

'Of course,' he laughed. 'You are cousin of Marduka, the officer of the palace gate.'

'How do you know this?' she queried, her heart beating frantically.

'Artaynte and I discovered it written in the records last night. Harbona investigated the matter of the attempted assassination fully for me.'

'You do not hate the Jews?'

'Hate them?' He frowned. 'Of course not. My great grandfather set them free from bondage and gave them permission to return to their homeland and my father helped them a great deal by giving them gold for their temple at Jerusalem. I have no other people in my whole Empire who are so loyal and law-abiding.'

'Then why are we sentenced to death?'

Khshayarsha stared at her in disbelief. 'Child, you have been at the wine too early in the day. I have not sentenced them to death. I would never do such a thing.'

'But,' she trembled at his accumulating rage. 'But the proclamation....'

The King's dark eyes closed to slits. 'Proclamation? What proclamation?'

Astur suddenly looked puzzled. 'The proclamation to have all Jews executed. If it had been that we had been simply sold into slavery, I would not mention the matter. We have been in slavery before so it would be nothing new. But now, we have been sentenced to death. Not just my people, but I, too.'

'No-one will harm you. He who harms you harms me and I

shall not stand for such an act of treason.'

Astur's eyes lifted slightly as Haman walked in, smiling and bowing to all the exalted company in the room.

'Then, my Lord King,' she said, raising her voice slightly. 'I regret to say you have been deliberately deceived in this matter.'

The King stood up, blind rage clear in his face as the whole room fell silent. 'Who would dare do such a thing?' he bellowed at her. 'Tell me at once.'

Haman hadn't heard the start of the conversation but he knew enough from the look Astur was giving him that something was gravely amiss.

'The man who would kill your Queen and all her family, the one who would seek to bring personal damage to the one we call in Hebrew "Ahasuerus, King of Kings",' she pointed, 'Is that wicked man, Haman.'

The King mouthed the name slowly as he backed towards the open window leading to the palace garden. Harbona and the others rushed to help their King who was obviously in considerable mental and emotional distress.

Alone, Haman gaped at Astur. 'You are a Jew?'

The Queen nodded. 'I am cousin and adopted daughter of Marduka.'

'The girl from the river,' he whispered hoarsely. 'You are the one my sons told me about. The one who got away.'

Astur frowned. 'Your sons?'

'No, I didn't mean...' he began, suddenly realising he had already said too much.

'So that's it,' she said slowly as full realisation dawned on her. 'Like father, like sons.'

'What are you going to do?' he asked with a glance towards the open window.

Astur was not about to relent. 'You have plotted against my people, Haman, and deliberately deceived your King. You and your sons will pay with your lives.'

'But why my sons?'

'Because they are like their father, Haman. I was there when they murdered my father in cold blood, when they raped my mother, over and over again, while she pleaded for mercy. Your sons showed no mercy, Haman, and neither shall I.'

Astur slipped her feet to the floor but Haman towered over her menacingly. 'I cannot let you do this.'

'Are you going to kill me, too, Haman?' Ignoring his attempts to intimidate her, she stood up, her face inches from his as she looked him straight in the eye. 'Or are you going to rape me first? It seems to be the only thing your family is any good at.'

As she turned from him, Haman instinctively grabbed at her and the gown slipped from her shoulder as they both lost their balance and fell back onto the couch. It was the wrong moment for the King to return.

'What is this?' he bellowed in uncontrolled rage. 'Have you not already done enough to my Queen? Do you dare also to try and abuse her on her own couch? Right here, in my presence?'

Haman leapt away from Astur as if she was red hot and shook his head frantically, his protests of innocence choking in his throat.

'Take him away,' the King commanded and the palace guards grabbed Haman's arms and jerked him to his feet.

Harbona leant close to the King. 'With respect, Your Majesty. I have unearthed this document.' Like some kind of court magician, Harbona produced with a flourish the death warrant originally meant for Marduka. 'This Marduka saved your life, my Lord King, and Haman would have hung him today from the stake he has had erected, fifty cubits high.'

Gradually, the rage dissipated from the King's face as everyone paused with baited breath. Khshayarsha suddenly nodded with inspiration. 'You men. Take this animal outside to the public square and hang him on this stake of his. Ensure everyone in Shushan sees it.'

Harbona covered Haman's face before the guards dragged him, screaming and pleading, from the room. Khshayarsha then relaxed and turned round to see his Queen in the arms of his son, crying her eyes out.

'Take good care of your step-mother, Darius,' he said kindly. 'For the next few months, Astur will need every bit of help we can give her.'

GRADUALLY, order in the room returned to normal as Harbona returned from having completed his duty. Behind him, Marduka arrived, dressed in the clothes which Haman had used to display him to the city. He bowed low before the King.

The King stood up once more. 'Marduka, son of Jair, you have served me well. From now on, you shall have the house and position of Haman at the Queen's bequest. I need someone I can trust as Prime Minister and I believe that you are that man.'

Harbona placed an object in Mordecai's palm. 'Take this seal-ring. Whatever you command shall be the word of the King and Ahura-Mazda.'

'It is a great honour,' said Mordecai as Astur slipped her arm through his.

'With you two beside me,' smiled Khshayarsha. 'It is I who am honoured. In the history of the Persians and Medes, none have served their king with greater loyalty.'

'It is our duty,' said Mordecai. 'Our God has decreed that, one day, we will again have a Kingdom of our own. But until then, we shall all continue to serve you faithfully.'

'If we live,' said Astur quietly.

'Yes,' said Khshayarsha thoughtfully. 'We must find a way to overcome the law I was tricked into passing.'

'With respect, my Lord King,' spoke up Harbona. 'Much as it grieves me to say so, the law is unchangeable and, therefore, cannot be reversed.'

'Maybe not,' said the King thoughtfully, 'but perhaps there is another way. Marduka, can your people fight?'

'If they have to, your Majesty. They would not use arms against you, but self-defence would be a different matter.'

'Very well. Put through an order in my name that, on the day decreed by Haman, the Jews are permitted to defend themselves by whatever means are necessary. Instruct all the Princes and Satraps throughout the Empire to give your people any assistance that is needed.' He smiled. 'I would suggest you use Haman's gold reserves to buy-off any reluctant ones. Any plunder in the process will become yours, of course.' He smiled to his Queen and new Prime Minister. 'May your God go with you.'

THE next day, the scribes were busy again. In every language of the day, they copied out Marduka's carefully-worded decree and each document was sealed with the King's own seal-ring and issued to post-carriers to go to the length and breadth of the realm. Great consternation arose over some of the wording and Marduka continued to explain and clarify over the next few weeks as the ferocious summer heat forced the Court to retire to Ecbatana in the mountains.

A new kind of relationship had developed between Astur and Khshayarsha. This time, they went to the summer capital together and the Queen was shown the great palaces of the Zagros. The couple were virtually inseparable as all day-to-day matters were left to Mordecai and the other Princes. Only the really important issues of state were brought to the King's attention.

'Why did your cousin not insist on Haman's sons being executed?' the King asked one day as they strolled through the palace gardens. 'I have to say, if I had been Marduka, I would have had them all hung, their women ritually desecrated, and the children sold into slavery in Anatolia or somewhere equally remote.'

Astur bowed her head. 'Marduka acted at my request, my Lord King.'

Khshayarsha turned to face her. 'But they had not only encouraged their father in the dirty deed, they had actually killed your mother and father.'

'They had, I agree. But my memory tells me that there were also one or two who objected. If Marduka had had them all killed, the possibly innocent would have died with the guilty. Now, we shall leave the matter until we return to Shushan. Whichever of Haman's sons refuses to honour your counter-decree and insists on still attacking my people shows himself to be a rebel against your law. Then, he will surely deserve to die.'

Khshayarsha smiled. 'You've got it all worked out in your clever little mind, haven't you? I'm glad you are on my side.'

'I always will be, my husband. You are a wise ruler and your word can be trusted.' She changed the subject. 'Any news of Themistocles?'

'Yes. He has written only this week, requesting a year or so to learn the Persian language before coming to Elam.'

'A year will not make a lot of difference, will it?'

'Certainly not. Although, I admit, I am not entirely convinced that a further full-scale invasion of Greece is what I want right now. I am so happy to just be here with you and my loyal people. For the first time in decades, the whole Empire is at peace. War is an expensive business and wealth can be utilised for better purposes.'

'There are many who would disagree with you on that matter.'

'You are right, my dear. Megabyzus for one. It seems he is not happy unless he is suppressing some revolt or other. If I do not watch him carefully, I would not put it past him to start a revolt just so he can go and put it down again.'

Astur smiled. 'Surely he is not that bad.'

'He is not bad, Astur - simply young, inexperienced and headstrong. He thinks with his sword-arm instead of his head.'

Astur threw her head back and laughed aloud.

'It is good to hear such laughter. So many times, courtiers laugh to please me and I know they do not mean it but are simply afraid to disappoint me. I admit, at times, I would rather they be honest and genuine like yourself.'

'My Lord King,' said Astur, gripping his arm. 'You must be the wisest king who has ever ruled Persia.'

'Not the world?'

Astur hesitated. 'Israel did have a good King once. His name was Solomon and his God asked him what he needed to rule his kingdom, thinking he would ask for riches or glory. However, he asked for wisdom instead and it was granted him. King Solomon has written thousands of proverbs which are still quoted by wise men, even here in Persia.'

'Is there a way I could be as wise as this King?'

'You already have great wisdom, my Lord. You also have

something else.'

'And that is?'

'You have the power to apply the wisdom in a far greater way than Solomon ever had. You are King from India to Ethiopia. Prince Darius will have a lot to live up to.'

'Darius has empathy for people. I wonder sometimes if he will not be too soft.'

They walked through the archway into the great walled garden. 'If used well, a certain amount of leniency can go a long way.'

'Like you with Haman's sons?' said the King. He plucked the head from a flower in bloom and placed it in Astur's hair before continuing along the side of the ornamental lake.

'Exactly. Give them enough rope and they will hang themselves upon it.'

'Are you not worried about what will happen on the day Haman decreed by lot?'

'Not at all, my Lord King. I have every confidence that my people have the strength to defend themselves.'

'Some of my Princes are wondering if I have not given your people too much freedom by the counter-decree.'

Astur stopped suddenly. 'What do they fear?'

'That the Jews will unite and overthrow the Empire or at least part of it. They might try to say it is the arrival of this Kingdom of which you spoke earlier.'

Astur shook her head. 'They will not do that.'

Khshayarsha frowned. 'How can you be so sure?'

'Because it is not yet the time for this kingdom. Anyway, Marduka and I have written to the Jews forbidding any kind of rebellion.'

'Ah. But will they take notice of the Queen of the Persians?'

Astur's eyes flashed in the sunlight. 'They had better.'

KHSHAYARSHA propped himself up on one elbow and looked down at his wife, his hand resting gently on her warm belly.

'You really are something special,' he said with feeling.

Astur smiled. 'I am only here to please my Lord the King.'

'If only this idyllic situation could go on forever.'

The Queen frowned. 'Why can't it?'

'Nothing is forever, these days,' he sighed. 'Do you know? Of all the wives and concubines I have had, I have to admit you are the best. I don't know what it is, but you have something none of the others ever had.'

'We Hebrews call it *ahev*, my husband - love. It is not something which can be faked.'

'It is in the eyes,' he said and kissed her gently.

'If I have pleased you, my Lord King, might I ask a very great favour?'

'Of course, name it. Up to half my kingdom.'

Astur laughed. 'Have you not yet learned, Khshayarsha? I do not desire wealth and power, I simply long for the love of a good husband.'

He sighed. 'If only I could live up to your expectations.'

She sat up and touched his face tenderly. 'But you do. I could ask for no-one better.'

He looked down. 'What is your desire?'

'To appoint a new Maid of Honour to the harem.'

He frowned again. 'What is wrong with Artaynte? Has she displeased you?'

'Not at all. It is just... It is just that...'

'Yes?'

'She wishes to get married. With the King's permission, of course.'

Khshayarsha sat up straight. 'Artaynte? Marry? Whom?'

'My cousin, Marduka.'

'I thought a Jewish man could only take a Jewish woman for himself.'

'That is true but Artaynte wishes to become a Proselyte - to be adopted as a Jew.'

'Well, well,' he smiled. 'My little Artaynte.'

'You are not angry?'

'I shall miss her. She was a good girl.'

Astur laughed. 'My Lord King, you speak of her as if she is dead. You will still see her often. Is not Marduka your Prime Minister?'

'Whom would you choose as a replacement?'

'I would appoint one of the other maids - Melane of Nippur.'

'She is indeed beautiful in form.'

'Is it a deal?'

He nodded. 'If it is your wish. In some ways, I would like to do away with the harem completely. Those women are sometimes more trouble than they are worth.'

'Would I be enough to satisfy your desires?'

'It depends. A King needs love often.'

'That I would gladly give.'

He laughed. 'No woman loves her husband that much.'

'I do. But, even then, it would not be wise to disband the harem altogether.'

'And why not? If you will satisfy my every need, why do I need a harem? Why, I will not even need Melane.'

'But you will, my Lord King.' Astur looked sad. 'You see, I can give you my love but there is one thing I cannot give you.'

'And what is that?'

'A son.'

The King was silent for a long time before he spoke. 'How can you know this?'

'Apparently, I was damaged by my fall into the river whilst trying to escape from Haman's sons. I have been to the physicians and they all agree. I am unable to produce children.'

'But physicians can be wrong.'

'They often are. However, have you not noticed that I am not as other women?'

'Not that I've noticed. Everything seems to be in the right place.'

'Externally, yes. What you may never have noticed is that I do not have a normal menstrual cycle. I am incapable of conceiving a child. They mentioned lots of big words about parts of the body I did not understand but the message came loud and clear. I was to be forever barren.'

'Astur,' he said gently. 'I had no idea.'

'Do you not understand? That is why I had to flee from the palace. Your attendants indicated that you wished to keep me, one day to become your Queen. I could not disappoint you in that way.'

'And that is why you kept yourself locked away in the gatehouse for so long?'

'Yes,' she bowed her head. 'However, I was with Artaynte and her love, I'm afraid, was infectious. When Artaynte and Marduka persuaded me to present myself before you, I hesitated at first for what I thought were moral reasons. Even when I agreed, I convinced myself that you had other concubines who could bear you children.'

'Is this why you do not wish me to disband the harem? You are still thinking only of me?'

She bowed her head. 'Yes. You see, I still love you and want, above all else, for you to be happy.'

'And you want me to take on Melane?'

'Melane is part of a large family. Her mother seems to

produce children simply when her husband glances at her so I feel that Melane will be equally as fertile and will produce a great many fine sons for you.'

He smiled. 'Then it shall be as you have spoken. Artaynte may marry your Marduka, and Melane will bear my children.'

THE King awoke to bird song and turned over to find that he was alone. He frowned, rose from the bed and went to the window. Everything looked so normal. And yet, for some inexplicable reason, he felt uneasy.

'Harbona,' he called and the attendant arrived quickly. 'Where did the Queen go? Did you see?'

'Yes, my Lord King.' He bowed. 'She left with her maids.'

'Left? Out of the city?'

'Why, yes, my Lord King. As always.'

He reached for his gown. 'Send Megabyzus to me.'

'Yes, my Lord King.'

His son-in-law arrived shortly. 'You called, my father?'

'Yes. I need to know where it is that the Queen goes each morning. Can you find out?'

Megabyzus smiled. 'I already know that. She goes up there.' He pointed north-east to where the stark, barren peaks of the Zagros stood clear of the treeline.

'Up there? Up the mountain?'

'Every day. I have had the three of them followed a few times but, alas, I have no man who can keep up with them.'

'What do you mean?'

'They run, Sire.'

'Run? Are you insane, Megabyzus?'

'Not at all. When my men reported back to me, I too, disbelieved. But, every morning, the Queen collects Artaynte and Melane and they run up the mountain. It takes them over an hour to reach the top and a little less to come down. I keep thinking that, one day, they will fall. However, it appears they are all extremely nimble of foot.'

The King glanced at the nearby peak. 'Are they meeting someone up there? Someone who could do us harm?'

'I do not think so. They are not up there long enough. They merely go up and then come down again.'

'I will find out today what this is all about.'

Megabyzus smiled. 'As you wish, sire.'

Khshayarsha dressed and walked along the balcony and, as he began to descend the stone steps, he saw the three girls enter the gate and disappear into the doorway to the courtyard of the women. Mystified, he followed and gently pushed open the door. The three of them were in the bathing pool.

'Good morning, my Lord King,' called Astur as she saw Khshayarsha. 'You may come in. It is but we three who are here.'

Suddenly, he was feeling foolish. Despite Astur's devotion to him, he had half-suspected she was up to something.

'What have you been doing?' he heard himself ask.

'Exercise, My Lord. It was Hegai's idea.'

'Hegai?'

The Queen smiled as Melane splashed water over her shoulders. 'On the night you and I were to be wed, he gave me some sound counsel. He said "If you want to keep your king, keep your tongue, but if you want to keep your man, keep your figure." I have never forgotten his words.'

Khshayarsha laughed. 'That sounds like good advice to me.'

'At first, I didn't think so. However, in time, he was proved to be right. Every day, he made me run seven times round the palace at Shushan.'

'But why do you have to go outside the city? It could be dangerous, especially up there.'

'Alas, here in Ecbatana, it is not possible to run around the palace. So, as next best thing, we run up the mountain.'

'To keep your figure?'

'You don't think I would stay looking like this for long if all I did was sit around and eat, do you?' She slipped a towel around her shoulders only and stood before her King. 'Do you not approve?'

He looked her up and down. 'Of the figure? Yes. Of the running? I'm not so sure. You could get attacked or lost or something.'

'Attacked? Lost?' laughed Astur. 'With Megabyzus' guards trying to keep pace with us all the time? Fat chance of that.'

'So you know?'

'Of course. Your son-in-law should train his men better. If we ever got attacked, I think we would end up protecting our guards instead of the other way round.'

The King smiled. 'You are probably right. We need a good war to get the men back into shape. They are getting lazy.'

'Well, we most certainly are not,' she said cheekily and then kissed him briefly. 'Now, are you going to join us in the pool? Or will you allow us to get dressed?'

Khshayarsha shook his head. 'It's a good job that I can trust you.'

Astur grinned. 'It is, isn't it?'

THE Court was back in Shushan as the heat began to dissipate and arrangements were well under way for the wedding of Mordecai to Artaynte. The King had granted unlimited funds to Astur but Mordecai had insisted on a simple Jewish wedding to whom all the Israelites in Shushan were invited as well as the members of the King's household. After the relatively simple ceremony, Astur held a banquet for them all in the palace garden.

'Your people are a good people,' remarked Khshayarsha as he watched them dance and sing. 'What is it that makes them so happy?'

'It is a mixture of faith and hope. As they hear the reports of the continuing construction of the temple in Jerusalem, it makes them joyful to know that their relatives in Israel are at peace.'

'But don't they realise that, within a few weeks, they will be fighting for their lives?'

'Of course, my Lord King. But their hope is in their God who promises He will protect them.'

'Do you, too, have this hope?'

'Naturally. I have every confidence in my God.'

'Astur,' he said quietly. 'Your faith and hope are infectious.'

'You are not the first Achaemenid king to speak those sentiments. Your grandfather, Cyrus was very impressed with Daniel and others as was your father, Darius.'

'One day, your people will rule the world.'

'It was so promised to our father, Abraham. God said his seed would fill the earth like the sands of the seashore.'

'But will they always be so happy?'

'I hope so, my Lord King.'

'When they are finished dancing, you must bring Marduka and Artaynte to me. I wish to bless them.'

Astur looked astounded for a moment but complied with the King's request. A few moments later, the newlyweds stood before their monarch.

'Marduka, I owe you my life. Artaynte, I owe you much of

my present happiness. Astur, I owe you my future. I wish to place my blessing upon you all. May my words go into the record books as the law of Ahura-Mazda.'

Harbona sat down beside the King and waited with writing block poised.

'Marduka. I hereby decree that, from henceforth, you will permanently remain Prime Minister of Persia and that the position will be hereditary. Artaynte, you will be the mother of all future Prime Ministers.'

'It is a great honour, your Majesty.'

'Astur. From this day forward, you will be my equal in power. When I offered you power and riches, you turned them down as did your King, Solomon. For that reason, you will be Queen, not just in name, but in fact. If I die, you must be co-ruler with my son.'

'You will not die,' said Astur. 'Not for a very long time.'

'It has to happen one day, my child. I do not decree that you marry Darius, only that you share the rulership with him to help him in his young years. You have a wisdom second only to that of your Solomon.'

'You are most kind, my Lord King.'

'From now on, there will be a council of three which will settle all immediate matters in court. Let it be written that the King, Queen and Prime Minister will make up that council and all others will be inferior except in the matter of war where all Princes must be consulted, as before.'

'It is so written,' said Harbona.

'Well,' said the King to Marduka and Artaynte. 'What are you waiting for? Go and enjoy yourselves.'

Astur gripped the hand of her King. 'My Lord King. I, too, have a proclamation to make.'

The King's left eyebrow raised a little. 'Yes?'

Astur leaned close. 'I love you.'

She nodded to the perplexed Harbona with a cheeky grin on her face. 'So let it be written.'

AFTER having waited for almost a year, the twelfth month came upon them with unexpected speed. Throughout the realm, Anti-Semitists and opportunists prepared to attack the peaceful Jews while they in turn got ready to defend themselves. To many, it seemed like an omen so that, throughout the Empire, many Gentiles actually became Proselytes. Others, fearing the wrath of the King, chose to suppress their natural feelings and simply do nothing. Nevertheless, there were still many thousands who were prepared to fight to eradicate the Jews from their communities. Among them were Zeresh and the ten sons of Haman.

'You each know what to do?' asked their mother.

'Of course. We have been through it so many times. Dalphon and Poratha go for Marduka and his new woman. The others spread out around the city and lead the marches against the Jews.'

'It is important,' said Zeresh. 'Marduka must die. I owe it to the memory of your father.'

'And the Queen?'

She nodded and her eyes glinted in the light of the oil lamps. 'Oh, yes. The Queen must also die.'

'Will not the King protect her?'

'He cannot. In his ignorance, the document was issued to destroy all Jews, whoever they are. The counter-decree only says they can defend themselves. The King will have to remain neutral in the matter or no-one will ever accept his word again. He dare not intervene.'

'Who will do the deed?'

'I have spoken with Artabanus. He will find a way to smuggle me into the palace with your sisters, Amele and Darusana, dressed as maids. I have sworn before Molech to avenge Haman or die. We will be the ones who will hold down the Queen while Artabanus deals with her. If we fail, we will bring upon ourselves the fate intended for the Queen. We have so sworn it.'

'Then let us hope you succeed.'

'My son,' said Zeresh. 'I have no intention of failing.' She smiled. 'You see, I have become quite attached to my belly.'

ASTUR rose carefully from her bed and, slipping her gown over her body, tiptoed out of her chamber. Quickly, she ran along the passageway and into the entrance hall.

'Your Majesty?' said the guard.

'I won't be long. I am going to see Marduka.'

'I will accompany you,' said the Captain, knowing full well what would happen to him if the King found out she was allowed into the city unguarded, on this of all days.

'Very well,' Astur sighed. 'But quietly, please.'

Together, they slipped through the shadows until they reached the gate. In a matter of an hour or so, the sun would be up but, in the meantime, the night seemed full of shadows. Four of them seemed to be heading for the palace.

'Captain,' she whispered. 'I think those people intend to attack the King. You had better follow them and make sure they are able to do no harm.'

Without further thought, the Captain nodded and went after them, keeping to the deepest shadows. Astur smiled, ran out of the gateway and knocked on the big door at the end of the street.

'It is Hadasseh,' said Astur as the small inspection panel opened. The door opened and she went inside.

'You took a risk coming here,' said Artaynte with concern.

'No more than staying at the palace. At least, here, we are together.'

The girls embraced as Mordecai entered. 'So you came.'

'I had to, my father. I wanted to be with you.'

'Very well.' He turned to his attendant. 'Congregate the servants, at once.'

Within minutes, Mordecai's entire household was gathered before him.

'My friends, today is the day when many will seek to kill me and my brothers. You will notice that the Queen is also with us and that her life, too, is in grave danger. I cannot expect you to stay and risk your lives with us and therefore give you freedom to leave whenever you wish. Return to your families and friends until this is all over.'

They stood in silence for a long time until an elderly man stepped forward. 'I know I have served you but a matter of months, my Lord Marduka, but I am too old to leave now, especially as I have nowhere else to go.'

Artaynte's maid stepped forward. 'I will stay with my mistress and die with her if need be.'

'I, also,' said the butler, then the cook and, eventually, the whole household.

Mordecai had tears in his eyes as he thanked them.

'The Queen will not die,' said the groom grasping a sword which seemingly materialised out of nowhere. In a matter of minutes, all the servants had armed themselves with anything they could lay their hands on and, as the sun rose over the Zagros, they were ready.

ALMOST instantly, there came the sound of fighting from all over the city. They waited in the house until there came the inevitable banging at the door.

'Come out or we will burn down the house with you in it,' called Dalphon.

Astur recognised the voice immediately; the voice she had not heard in many years; the voice of the first man to rape her mother.

'Let them in,' she said quietly and the butler glanced at Mordecai for confirmation.

Mordecai nodded and the door was opened and about a dozen men strode in with swords and spears.

Dalphon stopped and his mouth dropped open at the sight of Astur. 'You are here?'

She confronted him. 'Of course. This is where I should be. I am afraid your mother and sisters have a little shock in store for them at the palace.'

'You mean...?'

'I mean that they are now my prisoners. If I do not return to the palace, safe and sound, they will be executed.'

'You wouldn't do it.'

'How dare you come here in this manner and attempt to kill my relatives and friends?' She stepped close to him, her face inches from his. 'I know how they intended to dispose of us. They want to do it in the same way you tortured my mother.'

He looked puzzled. 'Your mother?'

'Do you not remember, Dalphon? Nor you, Poratha? Have both of you already forgotten the woman on the road from Babylon who begged you for mercy? Did you not hear her cries when she pleaded with you not to harm her unborn child? I do, because I was there. I heard it and, that day, I swore I would see you die for what you did.'

A look of stark fear flashed across his face as Astur spat the words at him. He opened his mouth the speak but, instead, grunted.

Astur pushed again and the blade in her hand went deeper. 'Do you remember now?'

The other men stood, as if paralysed, as Dalphon slowly sank to his knees. Gradually, the servants encircled the other terrified invaders and, before they could flee, they were all struck down. Artaynte put her arms around the trembling Queen.

'I have killed a man,' moaned Astur.

'You have executed a criminal,' consoled Artaynte. 'Is that not right, Mordecai?'

'He was a rapist and a murderer, Astur,' agreed the Prime Minister.

'Also,' added Artaynte. 'There is the King's decree that Jews could defend themselves. You are a Jew and have defended not only yourself, but your family and friends.'

'It is God's law, my child,' added Mordecai. '"An eye for an eye, a soul for a soul". With the death of Dalphon and Poratha, you have avenged the lives of your father and mother as well as that of the unborn child.'

Astur raised her head. 'It is as you say, my father.' She paused. 'I must return to the palace.'

'I will accompany you,' said Mordecai.

'And me,' said Artaynte.

Together, they scurried towards the palace as screams and cries emitted from buildings all around them.

The Captain of the Guard met them. 'I have taken the prisoners, your Majesty.' He beamed with pride. 'There were three women.'

Astur sighed. Only the women were caught. 'Take me to

them.'

The Captain led the way along the passageway until he came to the room near the Court of Women. He unlocked the door and stepped aside as the Queen breezed past him. Astur stopped and put her hand to her mouth. Frantically, she fought to hold back the bile in her throat as she surveyed the gory scene before her.

'Don't go in,' said Astur as Artaynte tried to see. She turned on the Captain of the Guard. 'Who did this vile act?'

'Your Majesty. They were alive when we put them in there and locked the door.'

'Some death,' said Astur, shaking her head to clear it. 'That is what they intended for me. Zeresh meant for me to see this as a sign.'

'A sign of what?' said Marduka.

'Whoever is behind all this wants me humiliated and desecrated as was my mother.' She bowed her head. 'It is the sign of how I am to die.'

FOR two days, the fighting went on. In Shushan alone, eight hundred people died and, over the next few weeks, reports were to come in concerning the deaths of over seventy-five thousand who had sought to kill the Jews but had been defeated.

When all the hue and cry died down, Astur went before the King. 'With your permission, my Lord King, I would have the bodies of Haman's ten sons hung up in the public square as a deterrent against future conspiracies within the Empire.'

'It is your right, Astur. They killed your mother and sought to kill you and your family.'

She turned. 'Harbona, would you see to the matter?'

'At once, your Majesty.'

As the attendant left, Astur gestured to a young man in the doorway. 'I wish to introduce my relative, Nehemiah, from Babylon. He has brought you the plunder from the activities of recent times.'

'But that is for you Jews. I have given my word.'

'And I have given mine,' said Astur. 'In my proclamation, I gave my people permission to defend themselves but all the spoils must come to the wise King who acted in their behalf.'

He stared at the huge mass of wealth being dumped before him. 'I am without words.'

'Then you will accept this gift from my hand?'

'It would be rude of me to refuse but I am still overcome.'

Astur laughed. 'Then send it to Artakhshayarsha at Persepolis. It will buy many bricks and columns for your new palace.'

'It will indeed. How can I thank you?'

'By allowing my people opportunity to celebrate their deliverance by an annual festival. To time indefinite, we shall remember the day when we were to be killed but, because of the power of our God and the wisdom of our King, we survived.'

'It was not I who saved your people, Astur. It was you. This, by rights, should all be yours.'

'What is mine is yours, my Lord King.'

'Then write to your people as you have spoken. Command them to celebrate those days of deliverance.'

It was at that moment that Harbona returned. 'My Lord King. Sataspes has returned from Egypt.'

The King smiled. 'Show him in. I must have news of his voyage around Africa.'

The young man was shown in and his father accompanied

him. Sataspes bowed before the throne. 'My Lord King, I have completed the journey.'

'Excellent. I have received reports from time to time of your progress. You must tell me of the Red Sea and the canal my father built across to the Nile.'

'Well...er...I'm afraid I didn't get that far.'

'What? Then how did you get home?'

'We...we turned round and sailed back up the west coast of Africa. I have a great many tales to tell of...'

'Enough! You have tricked me, Sataspes.'

'Tricked you, sire?'

'In return for your life, you promised to circumnavigate Africa and sail up the Red Sea. You have not completed your side of the bargain.'

'But it was the weather, your Majesty. It was very stormy.'

'Stormy? The storms haven't stopped the Greeks, have they? According to Themistocles, they are planning to send ships as far as the land of Thule and, eventually, explore the whole world. I thought at least you were man enough to explore the coasts of Africa. Instead of a man, I've got a woman who is afraid of the wind.'

'I tried, your Majesty.'

'You are making a fool of me, Sataspes. I gave you your life on the condition you would do as I asked. Did you think I would break my own law?'

'But, Sire,' interrupted Artabanus. 'My son will not repeat his foolishness with Artaynte.'

'No, he won't. I don't think her husband would like that.'

'Husband?' gaped Sataspes. 'Artaynte is married?'

'Married to my Prime Minister, Marduka. Perhaps I should ask him for his view on the subject. What say you, my Queen?'

Astur dragged her eyes from watching Artabanus who had a

strange expression upon his face. 'I say your word must remain, my Lord King.'

Artabanus stared at Astur with cold eyes and even Khshayarsha was taken aback by her sudden negative judgement.

'Sataspes had his chance,' continued Astur. 'But he chose to deliberately disobey his King. According to the law, my Lord King, you have no option.'

'Very well,' agreed Khshayarsha. 'Harbona, take him away.'

'No!' roared Artabanus. 'I will not let you do it.'

'How will you stop me?' asked the King.

Artabanus stared at his nephew for a long time but the King was adamant. Sataspes was taken away and Artabanus followed.

'I do not trust Artabanus,' said Astur quietly.

'He is an old man, Astur. He can do me no harm.'

'I hope and pray that you are right.'

ASTUR wrote the letter of command to all Jews in the Empire of the Medes and Persians. It read:

My brothers

It is with joyful heart that I write to you today to thank you for your support during the recent anti-Semitic activity sponsored by Haman the Agagite. I wish to confirm to you that the great King of Kings, known as Ahasuerus in the Hebrew tongue, knew nothing of the plot and has since done everything within his power to correct the situation and to help our people as did his father before him. As per my specific instructions, please ensure that all plunder collected from those who tried to eliminate us is handed over to the local satrap or to his representative for distribution. For this reason, people will never be able to say that we became rich because of an Agagite who had been cursed of God.

It is my wish and, I believe, the wish of our God, Jehovah of Armies, that we remember those days to times indefinite. Let it forever be remembered that Haman looked into the stars and cast the pur, the lot, and acted on behalf his god, Molech. Also let it be remembered with joyfulness that our God acted on our behalf and saved us from the wicked Haman and from the Devil who would seek to destroy the nation of God. It is the express command of the great King Ahasuerus that you be allowed to celebrate this festival of the pur, or Purim, each year. As the King has spoken, so let it be done.

Hadasseh Queen of the Persians

THE two men met at dusk on the outskirts of the city.

'It must be tonight,' said the older one.

'But Artakhshayarsha in at Persepolis. It will be better if they are all together.'

'I have taken enough, Megabyzus. If you are not with me, I will do it alone but, if I am to do it alone, you will not become my Commander-at-Arms.'

'I will do it, my Lord Artabanus,' said the younger man reluctantly. 'You can rely on me.'

'I hope so. I have seen too many attempts fail. Bigthana and Teresh had to go and get caught. Haman got his timing all wrong and misjudged Marduka completely. Even Zeresh broke into the palace at the very time the Queen was out in the city. This time, we must get it right. Do I make myself quite clear?'

'I will do just as you have commanded.'

'Good. Remember, you take care of Darius. Make sure he dies quietly else we will not be able to throw the blame on him later.'

'What of the Prime Minister and his wife?'

'We can deal with them later. First, I will deal with the King and then I can concentrate on his pretty little Queen.'

'You really do hate her, don't you?'

'Yes, I do. She has repeatedly humiliated me over these last few years and she was largely responsible for the execution of my son, Sataspes. Oh, yes. I hate her all right.'

'And then you will be King.'

'Yes,' he smiled. 'Then I will be King. You will take the Immortals to Persepolis tomorrow so that Artakhshayarsha can meet with an "accident". Then, nothing can stop us.'

Megabyzus also smiled. 'Nothing at all.'

THE Queen stirred restlessly in her bed. It was not often that it rained in the Euphrates-Hiddekel basin but when it did, it did so with a vengeance. Lightning lit up the chamber as Astur got to her feet and looked out at the downpour which fell in sheets past the arched window. In the courtyard below, figures moved and she frowned as such movement at so late an hour. She didn't know why she was so on edge, something had woken her but she knew not what it had been. Perhaps it was the call of some animal, frightened by the thunder which rolled without let-up along the Zagros.

Astur smiled. She was glad Khshayarsha would be happy tonight. During the evening, she had developed a headache which she had put down to the oppressiveness of the atmosphere before the storm and, as a last-minute change of plan, she had offered Melane as a substitute. Astur knew that her young maid had the youth and vitality to draw out the best from her husband and king.

Realising that sleep would no longer be possible, Astur threw the blue gown around her shoulders and stepped out into the corridor. She paused. Further down the hall, she could hear voices in hushed conversation. Frowning, she stepped quietly towards the royal chamber and noticed that the door was ajar. Khshayarsha would not be happy about being disturbed at so late an hour. The matter must be very urgent indeed to require his attention at this time of night.

Creeping towards the open doorway, she peered through. It was dark inside the room but she could just make out the shapes of several people who were gathered around the bed. Suddenly, there came the sound of a muffled scream which seemed to go on forever as she tried to make out what was happening. She stood, petrified, as she realised the sound had to be coming from her maid. As the screaming gradually died away, the men muttered and laughed softly amongst themselves before releasing their victim and walking towards the doorway. Instinctively, Astur ducked behind the long curtains and held her breath as they passed by less than a cubit from her.

'Let us see if Megabyzus has dealt with Darius,' came the voice she recognised instantly. 'If he has, he can leave immediately for Persepolis and then I will go and take care of Marduka.' He laughed to the other men. 'You men can have his woman if you want her.'

Astur shook with terror as they passed her by. Surely not, she thought. Please let it not be so. As the voices retreated down the passageway, she rushed to the bedside and grabbed Khshayarsha by the arm. The light was poor but she could see that he seemed to be sleeping so peacefully, a broad smile upon his face. Melane must have pleased him well, she thought.

The King didn't stir, even when she shook him frantically. It was then that she noticed the small dark patch on the front of his nightshirt. Stifling a scream, she peeled back the garment and saw the deep incision under his ribs. The King was not breathing.

She wanted to run, to hide, to wake up from her nightmare but, instead, stood and stared at the man she had loved so dearly. Her eyes drifted to Melane and, as they became accustomed to the dark, she saw that her maid was on top of the bed and that a pillow had been placed over her face. Carefully removing the pillow, she then saw the gaping mouth, the staring eyes and knew by the frozen expression that Melane had not died from being suffocated by the pillow.

Carefully, she reached over to the table and struck the tinder to light to a candle. With the dim flame to guide her, she turned back to the bed and almost dropped the light. It seemed that she had been thrown back eight years in time as she stared at the scene before her and realised that what she could see had been intended for her.

MORDECAI woke at the hammering at the door. Artaynte touched his arm. 'What is it?'

'I will go and see,' said the Prime Minister, slipping on his robe.

As he descended the stairs, the butler opened the door and Astur rushed in, soaked to the skin, still in her night gown.

'You must leave,' she cried. 'Artabanus is coming for you.'

'Leave? Artabanus? What are you saying, my child?'

'The King is dead!'

'Dead? The King?'

'Father, stop repeating everything I say. Artabanus has murdered Khshayarsha and is now on his way for you and Artaynte.'

'Then we must warn Darius and Megabyzus.'

'Too late. For whatever reason, Megabyzus has thrown his lot in with Artabanus. I think he believes his great-uncle will live up to some promise of power or riches. He obviously does not know him very well.'

'Then Prince Darius?'

'Killed by Megabyzus.'

Marduka reached for his cloak. 'We must warn Artakhshayarsha.'

'But he is at Persepolis, supervising the work on the palace.'

'Someone must go and tell him.' He turned to his butler. 'Go at once. Get the post-rider.'

'As you say, Lord Marduka.'

The butler left and Artaynte came down and put her arms around her friend. 'How did you get away?'

Astur bowed her head. 'They think I am dead.'

'But how?'

'Melane took my place tonight with the King. They murdered her, too.'

'Artabanus took her for you?'

'It was very dark. He... he disembowelled her alive.'

Artaynte gasped. 'Like Haman's sons did to your mother and Amestris did to mine.'

'Sarah was a good woman,' reflected Marduka.

'And so was Melane,' cried Astur. 'She was only seventeen and had seen virtually nothing of life.'

'We must think of the future,' interrupted the realistic Artaynte. 'You must get away from here before Artabanus realises his mistake.'

'So must you. They will come for you both soon.' She looked sadly at her friend. 'You have been promised to the guards.'

Artaynte swallowed. 'I would die first.'

'Mordecai will die first. I think they mean you to die afterwards, when they have used you to their satisfaction.'

'We will all leave,' announced Mordecai. 'We will go together.'

'Where?' asked Artaynte. 'Where could we go where we would be safe?'

'Eventually, we will go to Israel,' said Mordecai firmly. 'But, in the meantime, we will hide in the mountains until they have finished searching for us.'

'We will hide on the other side of the mountains,' smirked Artaynte. 'They will never find us there.'

'The Kavir?' gasped Mordecai. 'No-one has ever survived the Dasht-Kavir.'

'I know the salt-wastes. My father and I crossed them several times when I was a child.'

'It is suicide to go there. The Kavir is uncharted and without permanent form.'

'Then they will not find us, will they? We will bide our time and they will believe us to be dead.'

'I will meet you there,' said Astur thoughtfully as the post-rider arrived.

'Why?' said the astonished Mordecai. 'Are you not coming with us?'

She shook her head. 'There is something I must do first.'

'Something more important than saving your life?' gasped the frantic Artaynte.

Astur nodded. 'I must go to Persepolis.'

'Persepolis? But that is far out of your way.'

'It must be I who will warn Artakhshayarsha.'

'But you don't even like him.'

'Still, I must warn him. It is my duty and I owe that much to him. I loved Khshayarsha and so must now try to save his son.'

'But the post-rider will go.'

'Look,' reasoned Astur. 'If you were Artakhshayarsha and a post rider arrived with a message which told you that your father had been killed by his uncle and that your brother-in-law was on his way to assassinate you, would you believe it?'

Artaynte nodded. 'Probably.'

'Not without checking first, you wouldn't. Knowing the cautious Artakhshayarsha, he would send one of his own men to make sure before he acted and, if Megabyzus has already left for Persepolis, it would all be too late. I must get there first.' She turned to the patient post-rider, a young lad of about eighteen. 'Take off your clothes.'

The youth gaped at his Queen and then quickly slipped out

of the breeches and tunic which clearly identified him as a King's messenger. Astur discarded her nightgown and then slipped into the coarse material and pulled on the leather riding boots.

'Wait,' called Artaynte as her Queen turned to leave.

Astur turned and, suddenly, Artaynte was behind her with a sharp, bronze dagger in her hand. As Mordecai watched, his wife cut and hacked at the Queen and then stood back.

'Now, no-one will recognise you,' she said as she grinned at the short hair which now framed Astur's face.

'Yes, they will,' interrupted the messenger. 'With respect, Your Majesty, you are far too clean to be a post-rider.'

Astur laughed and bent down in the yard and smeared mud from the courtyard all over her face.

'Better?' she asked as she prepared to mount the specially-trained Arab stallion.

'Let him have his head, your Majesty,' advised the youth. 'Mercury loves to gallop hard.'

'Mercury,' repeated Astur as she held the reins tightly. 'I like that. Mercury, the flying messenger.'

'Take care, my little Hadasseh,' said Mordecai solemnly.

'Get out of here,' commanded the Queen before swinging her leg over the horse and disappearing into the dark and rain.

ASTUR did not know the road well but, fortunately for her, Mercury did and he galloped south-eastwards at full speed. Astur wiped the rain from her eyes and pulled up the hood of her cloak and lay low over the head of the magnificent stallion.

After only an hour, she ached all over. Her back was stiff from the strange position and her hands already sore from holding so tightly onto the reins. Also, the inside of her thighs were chafed from the rubbing against the hard saddle. She was soaked to the skin and feeling thoroughly miserable but she dare not stop. It was around three hundred miles from Shushan to Persepolis, a distance which would take Megabyzus and his cavalry almost four days to cover, even at full speed. Astur knew that she had to do it in less. Artakhshayarsha not only had to be warned, he would have to make preparations to defend the city against the invading army.

DAWN broke on Astur's left as she lay across the neck of her mount while he trotted along as if he had all the stamina in the world. The road was well-marked and the hoof-prints of the men ahead of her clearly visible in the sandy mud. The rain had abated to a fine drizzle and Astur had never felt so miserable in all her life.

The implications of what had happened were just coming home to her as she remembered that her husband was dead. Khshayarsha had not been the perfect ideal of a marriage partner and probably never would have been. Granted, he was a King and probably the richest man in the world but those things were not everything. She had always walked a tightrope and knew that if, one day, she did not fully please him, she would have been replaced just as surely as Amestris had been.

Astur was so deep in her thoughts and misery that she nearly rode right into the camp of Megabyzus. The cavalry had opted to call a halt for rest and food and Astur had rounded a corner north of Nasiri. It had been the low-throated grunt of Mercury which had made her look up and see them ahead. Standing up in the stirrups, she surveyed the terrain around her. To the south, the land was treacherous and marshy as wading birds strutted around looking for food. On her left, the sandstone seemed to rise almost vertically from the road, huge boulders seemingly poised ready to crash down upon her. Only the track they were on seemed safe enough to travel.

There was only one thing for it. Nudging Mercury forward at a slow walk, Astur edged her way towards their camp as the men ate and drank in the light mist that had gathered around them. Quietly and carefully, she approached the men until she could recognise some of them, Megabyzus sitting on a rock while others huddled under whatever shelter they could find. She was almost into the camp before they saw her. For a long time, no-one said a thing as the horse walked through their midst, Astur's heart beating frantically as she held her head down. In fact, she had almost reached the far side before one of them spoke.

'Where are you going, boy?' said Megabyzus, grabbing Mercury's halter.

'Ramuz, my Lord,' replied Astur in as deep a voice as she could muster.

'Don't I know you?' asked the Prince, his eyes mere slits as he peered at her and tried to put two and two together.

'I don't think so, my Lord,' she said with sudden inspiration. 'I have messages from Lord Artabanus to the Princes.'

'Very well,' he said, releasing her horse.

She trotted to the edge of the camp but couldn't resist the temptation to turn and look back. As she did, Megabyzus suddenly became suspicious as to why Artabanus would permit the news to get out before Artakhshayarsha had been captured and executed.

'Stop that post-rider,' came the command as Astur dug her heels in and galloped into the mist. Arrows fell to the roadway beside her but few came close as she let Mercury have his head.

The stallion was superb as she lay forward and held on tight.

Every time she glanced backwards, the chasing riders seemed a little further behind and, by high sun, she was alone in the foothills.

She had to stop soon, she knew. Even Mercury could not keep up that speed forever. Besides, her own body could only take so much punishment. Ahead lay the Zahreh valley as she topped the pass. She remembered the last time she had been here when Khshayarsha had pointed out various landmarks that could be seen from such a lofty elevation. She stopped and, jumping to the ground, tied Mercury's reins to a bush within reach of a swollen stream.

Without hesitation, Astur clambered up the craggy scree slope and stopped only where she had a complete view of the road ahead and behind her. In front, to the east, was the wide river she would need to follow all the way upstream for a great many miles until she was high among the tall, snow-covered peaks of the eastern Zagros. From where she stood, Kuh-e-Khayez was just visible to the east, its top sheathed in white cloud and, further south, the Mishim foothills. When Khshayarsha had brought her this way before, the caravan had followed the southern edge of the Zagros, via Shapur between the Mishim and the mighty Kuh-Tasak, one of the tallest of the south-eastern Zagros. During that long journey, the King had told her of another route, the high road of the Zagros, which ran close to the source of the Zahreh River. If she could make it up the steep valley, if at the top she could find this high road which might still be snowbound, if she could follow the road eastwards through the correct passes, then only could she descend into the wide, fertile valley below and then follow it downstream to Persepolis. It was very dangerous but, if she made it, it would cut several hours off her journey. If, if, if.

She turned and looked back at the way she had come. To the

west, she could see the Gulf of Parsa and the mouths of the Hiddekel and Euphrates Rivers. Further north could be seen the beginning of the wide, fertile valley that led to Babylon, the place of her birth. The road she had travelled lay beneath her, winding across the countryside and, not far away, the blur of many riders. The sight made up her mind for her. She had but one horse and, if it gave up, she would be alone and at their mercy. If, however, she could do the unexpected, take the road she had never travelled, she might just survive. Slithering down the scree, she recovered her horse who had drunk well and, after a sip herself, she nudged Mercury down the slope. At the bottom, the river was wide and deep from the melting snows of spring and Astur was glad she didn't have to cross it yet.

It was getting dark as she reached the tributary which followed the road to the right and she had to travel a long way upstream before she could find a safe place to cross the main river. On the far side of the raging waters, she almost fell from the saddle with exhaustion and found she no longer cared if Megabyzus caught up with her. She was able to travel no further so, settling down under an overhanging rock with the faithful Mercury standing guard, she immediately fell fast asleep.

WHEN Astur next opened her eyes, the sun was on her face. Stiff with sleeping on the ground, she sat up and peered outside at the morning. Her whole body seemed to ache from the riding she had not done for many years. Khshayarsha had forbidden his Queen to be seen on the back of a horse like a common wench and had insisted on her using the carriage. Her only exercise of late had been the running which, in itself, had not entirely equipped her for such a desperate ride.

She stared out at the hills around her and the nearby trees

that grew in the valley. Just a matter of yards away was Mercury, nibbling eagerly at the sparse grass on the hillside. A little further away was the tributary, hissing as it cascaded over the rocks. On the other side of the river was...Megabyzus.

She was suddenly wide awake as she rolled out of the hiding place, doing up the bronze catches on her tunic as she went. The army had not seen her even though it was camped just across that relatively narrow stretch of water. They had obviously ridden well into the night but had been reluctant to cross the torrent in the dark. However, it was now daylight and would not be long before they continued their journey. Silently, she crept from bush to bush until she was close to Mercury. She hesitated. One thing was certain. The moment she stood up and tried to mount her horse, they would see her and she was still well within arrow shot. Frantically, she looked around for inspiration. Due to the noise of the river, they would not hear her. If only she could distract them somehow. She only needed a matter of seconds and she would be out of range. After that, it would take them some time to cross the river.

Carefully, she untied the reins of her horse and moved as far as she could without detection. At the edge of the tree-line, she paused and placed her foot in the stirrup. She looked at the group of waders in the pool below and then tossed a rock into the water.

Instantly, there was pandemonium as the birds flew, squawking, into the air, terrified out of their minds. It would have taken some kind of superman not to glance in that direction and Megabyzus had none of those in his army. Astur was going full tilt down the hill away from them before they realised they had been tricked. Some of his men started to mount up but their leader realised the futility and called them back.

'We will catch the messenger in due course,' Megabyzus said with a smile. 'I don't yet know how he got past Artabanus but he will not get away from me. He has but one horse that cannot gallop forever.'

He selected a dozen men from his army of Immortals. 'Leave immediately and find him. When you bring his body to me, make sure it is in very small pieces.'

IT was late in the morning before Astur reached the spot where the roadway left the main river to follow the lower ground to Persepolis. She looked behind at the dust which relentlessly stayed on the horizon and realised that Megabyzus must have sent a squad of men after her as the main army, including supplies, could not have matched her speed.

Carefully, she rode Mercury across the water and up the far bank onto the stony road before wheeling the horse around and returning to the river. With satisfaction, she looked down at the score marks in the soft bank of the river and hoped that the men following her would be deceived. She then nudged her mount back into the water and waded upstream for more than a mile before climbing back out of the river and following the Rud-e-Zareh into the mountains.

As she climbed, the weather became colder. It was early spring and, by now, the temperature in Shushan would be almost unbearable. However, at so many cubits above the valley plain, Astur wished she had had the time and foresight to bring heavier clothing.

Already, it was getting late in the afternoon as she reached the fork in the river and debated which branch to take. Looking down the valley, she could see no riders.

However, it would not take the soldiers long to realise they had been fooled and, by now, they could already be tracing her steps or even trying to cut her off. It was probable that they knew these mountains far better than she did.

She stared up at the tall peaks ahead and made her decision. Abandoning the tributary on her left, Astur climbed the steep incline through the trees that followed the waterfall alongside her. At the top of the cascade, the waters came from two directions. Having chosen right before, she opted for left this time and broke out of the treeline onto a wild hillside scattered with broken rocks and the metamorphic debris of millennia.

It was the snow which made her turn back. It suddenly fell out of the sky like a solid wall and was then ferociously whipped around by the icy wind. In desperation and with heavy heart, she retraced her steps back to the trees where she sheltered until the light failed completely. For a long time, she stood beside Mercury who instinctively bowed his head against the ferocious gale. It was madness to continue. The storm might last for days and Megabyzus was on lower ground, able to make better speed.

Astur hung her head in shame. She had failed in her attempt to thwart the evil plans of Artabanus. The army would reach Persepolis ahead of her and the unsuspecting Artakhshayarsha would welcome Megabyzus with open arms and, by the time she reached the city, it would be all over. It would then be only a matter of time before the great dynasty of the Achaemenids was overthrown by nations who had accepted her husband's peace terms but who would not tolerate the deceit of Artabanus nor the bloodthirsty oppressions of Megabyzus. Soon, the whole world would be at war and it would simply be because the Queen of the Persians was now lost on the wild and snow-covered slopes of the High Zagros.

ASTUR had never seen so much snow before in all her life, not close up. Once, when she had been at Ecbatana, the distant peaks had been snow-capped and beautiful but she had never before felt its cold cloak envelope her whole body.

Deep into the night, she sat propped up against the trunk of an tree whilst the white flakes fell thickly from a black sky. Even in the dead of night, the mountainside seemed to glow. Under the great oak trees beneath which she sheltered, it remained relatively dry but Astur shivered from the unaccustomed cold. The wind had now died to a whisper and all was silent except for the soft patter of snow upon the leaves. From time to time, Astur looked towards where Mercury stood a few cubits away, pulling gently at what little there was of undergrowth. Should she let the horse go so it could return to the lower slopes where grass was more plentiful? Was it worth continuing her journey at all?

It was now too late for her to return to lower ground to find another way round. If she was still to reach Persepolis before Megabyzus, she would have to climb the snow-covered slopes in front of her and find the pass through the mountains without the aid of any footpaths which would, by now, be covered in a blanket, disguising every natural feature. Faintly, she could still hear the trickling of the nearby stream. Although the snow was settling, the temperature was not yet below zero, but it was not to last. After a while, the snow gradually ceased and the moon broke through the clouds and, as the night progressed, the temperature dropped. Astur's whole body seemed to be shaking from head to foot as she wrapped her arms around herself and tried to roll herself into a ball between the roots of the tree to try and conserve what little body heat she had.

Suddenly, she pricked up her ears as Mercury neighed softly

in the darkness. Instantly, she was onto her feet, holding her horse's head in her hands, straining for any repetition of the sound. But nothing disturbed the utter silence as even the trickling of the stream seemed to have died away. For a moment, Astur thought she had gone deaf but then Mercury moved slightly and Astur stood, poised, ready for action. The horse's eyes were wide and alert, its ears erect and scanning. Frantically, Astur's eyes peered into the darkness as her heart raced. Was it Megabyzus's men who were now close by and stalking her? She had no way of telling.

'Easy,' she whispered to Mercury as she stroked his nose reassuringly.

Astur was taking no chances. As quietly as possible, she leapt up and swung her leg over his back and gently patted his neck.

She looked around for options. Behind her, the forest loomed black and evil whilst ahead, at least she could see where she was going. A twig snapped somewhere and, with heart in mouth, she nudged Mercury forward. If whoever it was behind her was going to attack, it would be now.

As she moved, a great crashing broke out in the undergrowth to her rear. Instinctively, she dug her heels in hard and Mercury leapt ahead, stumbling through the crisp, white blanket. Astur looked wildly around and it was then that she saw the bear. It was big and black and catching up with them fast. Brutus was on his home ground whereas Astur was lost and Mercury weakened from the frantic riding of the last two days. Unable to see the terrain below the snow, the horse stumbled and Astur found herself flying over its neck.

The breath was forced from her as she hit the ground, the soft snow cushioning her fall somewhat. She shook her head as the mountain slowed down in its spinning and Astur stared up at the giant mountain bear which confronted her. Slowly, she got to her feet as the animal watched her warily, its panting tongue clearly seen in the moonlight. Even at a distance of several cubits, she could smell its breath, hot and stale, as the clouds of vapour condensed in the icy air.

Astur had no weapon except for her tiny dagger which was useless in these circumstances but she still did not fancy becoming the bear's next meal. She was on slightly higher ground, the animal's head being level with her own as its eyes followed her every move.

The bear was puzzled. Every other time it had attacked, its prey had run away only to be overtaken and, after a certain amount of mauling and bone-breaking, had been killed and pieces of it had been dragged back to the lair for food. However, this puny creature defied it. The bear, down-wind of her, sniffed the air and was puzzled at her lack of fear. Perhaps this skinny animal was stronger than she looked.

Astur felt no fear, merely disappointment that she had failed in her quest to save the Empire of her late husband and King. Then, she had an idea. Slowly, so as not to startle the bear, she bent down and picked up a large handful of snow and began to compress it into a hard ball in her hands. If little David could defeat big Goliath, it was just possible that Astur could escape Brutus.

She waited until the bear moved and, when it did, she threw the snowball with all her might, catching it full in the face. Brutus roared in anger and staggered to a stop, rubbing its eyes which had been blinded by the flying ice. Astur turned and ran, clutching Mercury's reins as she passed him and dragging him up the mountainside. They reached the top of the ridge as Brutus recovered and began bounding up the slope towards them. Astur jumped onto Mercury's back, dug her heels in and let the horse have its head as it raced along the level ridgeline and soon left the bear far behind. Several miles away, they stopped and Astur shivered violently as she tried to get her bearings, realising that she now had not the slightest idea where she was.

Dismounting, she stared up at the moon. What was it her father had taught her about navigation? As they had travelled across Mesopotamia, Abihail had pointed out the stars and the identifiable constellations and she frantically tried to remember what he had told her. The names Kesil, Kimah and Ash kept coming back to her but, as she looked up into the sky which seemed to be one solid mass of stars, she wished she had listened more carefully.

However, inspiration came suddenly. The moon, her father had once shown her, had a slight southerly bias. Like the sun, it rose in the east and set in the west. East was where she wanted to go so she tried to estimate the direction from which the moon had risen just an hour ago and, eventually, made something of what she saw. She reached a decision and only time would tell if she was right.

THE sun rose as Astur reached the end of the long ridge and began her descent of the rugged escarpment. The light was in her eyes so she knew she could not be far off the high road which led to Shiraz. As she broke free of the snow line and entered the tall trees hanging onto the southern edge of the Zagros, she saw, through the trees ahead, the wide marshes below her. Skirting them cautiously, Astur headed in what she estimated to be a north-easterly direction. Mount Karun, the source of Persia's greatest river, was straight ahead. Refreshed with water at Fathabad, Mercury raced ahead, his destination now in clear sight.

ARTAKHSHAYARSHA surveyed the scene before him at Persepolis. At last, the great doors of the great audience hall were hung in place. His father would be proud of what he had accomplished these last few months. When the King arrived next month for the New-Year celebrations, he would honour his youngest son with the great riches and glory he deserved.

A palace guard approached and bowed low. 'Your Highness, a post-rider has arrived from Shushan.'

'And?'

'He wishes to speak with you privately.'

'What cheek! Go back to this boy and tell him to give you his message or I shall have him flogged.'

The soldier bowed. 'At once, Prince Artakhshayarsha.'

Artakhshayarsha turned to his attendant. 'Do these people not know that no-one but myself and those I specifically authorise should see the palace before it is completed? If I showed everyone the defences, why all and sundry would know the secrets of our palace.'

Garan bowed respectfully. 'It is so written, your Highness.'

The guard returned. 'My apologies, Prince Artakhshayarsha, but the messenger stresses that the matter is of utmost urgency and he must speak with you and you alone.'

Artakhshayarsha grew angry. 'Does no-one listen to me?'

'Your Highness,' interrupted the guard. 'The messenger also claims to be her Majesty the Queen.'

Artakhshayarsha gaped and then stared towards the gate where, in the distance, her could see the small group of people beside the west gate of the city.

'Does this boy look like the Queen?'

'He is in the uniform of a royal messenger but looks a filthy ruffian, sire.'

Artakhshayarsha smiled. 'So, we have a comedian amongst

us, do we? Take this "queen" to the roof of the North Tower and have him stripped naked and then flogged in full sight of the entire army. When he begs for death, I will hear him out. Perhaps, then, I shall discover the truth of the matter.'

The guard grinned. 'You may leave it to me, sire.'

'Take your time over it. I have all day.'

The guard left and Artakhshayarsha returned to his work. 'Now where were we? With all these distractions, we will never be finished in time for my father's arrival.' He smiled. 'No-one will ever be able to accuse me of not obeying his laws to the letter.'

Garan bowed. 'You are a wise and honourable ruler, your Highness.'

The guard returned as they pored over the final plans. 'With respect, your Highness.'

'What is it now? Does the boy not bleed?'

'Sire, the messenger... is not a boy.'

Artakhshayarsha frowned. 'Not a boy?'

'We...er...stripped the messenger for whipping as you decreed and he is...she is...a woman.' He paused. 'My sergeant, Carnos, has been to the palace at Shushan. He thinks she may well be the Queen after all.'

Artakhshayarsha put down his chart. 'If this is some kind of joke, I will have you all flogged.'

He stormed off the platform and strode across the courtyard towards the North tower. Climbing the spiral stairway, he burst forth into the harsh daylight on the roof and stared down at all the people who were watching. Grabbing the whip from the guard, he stepped towards where Astur waited with her wrists lashed to a cross-bar above her head, her feet barely touching the ground. He grabbed her by the short hair and then stopped and stared into her eyes.

'Now I have seen it all,' he said quietly. He turned. 'Garan, release the Queen.'

'Thank you,' said Astur as they cut her free and she slipped her tunic back on.

Artakhshayarsha handed her a beaker of wine. 'This had better be good.'

Astur took it from his hand and sat down beside him. 'It is not good.' She placed her hand over his. 'Your father is dead.'

The youth jumped to his feet. 'Dead? How?'

'Murdered by Artabanus.'

'Then Darius...?'

'Killed by Megabyzus.'

'Then...?'

'Artakhshayarsha,' she said soberly. 'You are King.'

'King? But...?'

'And Megabyzus is now on his way here to kill you.'

'But why?'

'It has been written that you killed your father and brother to gain the throne.'

'But I was here, in Persepolis.'

'I know that and you know that, but how many will believe you and I? How many others know that you are innocent?'

'Why, Garan and the builders.'

'How many?' she persevered.

He shrugged. 'A hundred, perhaps.'

'You should know Artabanus by now. He will find a thousand witnesses who will claim they personally saw you assassinate your father and brother.'

'He would not dare.'

'Artakhshayarsha, there is a great deal at stake. Artabanus will stop at nothing to become King.'

'And Megabyzus...?'

'He will have been promised some high position. Alas, he does not know Artabanus well or he would not trust him.'

The Prince began to pace the tower. 'I will reason with him when he arrives here.'

'Somehow I think things have gone too far for that. Artabanus has the Immortals under his power and Megabyzus knows that. For the moment, he has no alternative but to go along with what your great-uncle has commanded.'

'We will defend the city.'

'With how many men?'

'Several hundred in total.'

'Megabyzus knows this and comes with a thousand. You will not stand a chance.'

'Then what do you propose?'

'I suggest that, for the time being, you hide out in the mountains.'

'With my army?'

'No. Leave them here to defend the city. Megabyzus will believe you are still here. Instruct your men to surrender only when defeat is imminent.'

'My men will never surrender,' interrupted Garan.

'I admire your bravery, Commander, but they must. When Megabyzus realises Artakhshayarsha is not here, he will spare you. He cannot risk alienating any of his army at the moment, not before the question of rulership has been completely settled. If, on the other hand, he arrives and finds the Prince still here, everyone will die as he will not risk leaving any witnesses.'

'Always assuming he breaks into the city.'

'He will, Commander. His life and the whole of his future are at stake. He will find a way to overthrow you.'

'How long before he gets here?' asked the Prince.

'I took a short-cut over the mountains but have gained only a few hours. He will be here before the day is out.'

Artakhshayarsha stopped before her. 'How do I know you are telling me the truth?'

'Have I ever lied to you?'

He contemplated for a moment. 'Not yet. But then, as you say, the stakes have never been so high.'

'I do not want rulership, Artakhshayarsha. If I did, I would not be here today, I would be in Shushan. I came because you are now King. You must escape and then find a way to reclaim your throne.'

'And what of you?'

'I will stay and face Megabyzus.'

'He cannot afford to let you live.'

'I know that. I am not afraid to die.'

'He will first torture you to try to find out where I have gone.'

'Megabyzus would be stupid not to, but I will not reveal the truth.'

'You will suffer great pain and humiliating deprivations.'

'So be it. I failed your father, so I deserve it.'

'You have made up for it by risking your life coming here.'

Astur shrugged. 'It will have been worth it if you become King. I will not have died in vain.'

'I cannot let you do it. I owe you my life. It is the law.'

'I release you from your obligation. Go, before Megabyzus arrives.'

The guard arrived. 'Sire. Riders approaching from the south.'

Artakhshayarsha stared out across the valley to where a distant cloud of dust heralded the approach of a large number of horses. He turned to Astur. 'Can you ride?'

'I rode here from Shushan, didn't I?'

Artakhshayarsha turned to the Garrison Commander. 'Garan, defend the city as the Queen has spoken. The Queen and I are leaving immediately.'

'Alone?'

Artakhshayarsha nodded. 'We will travel faster that way.' He turned to his attendant. 'Get me peasant clothes and a horse. And food for the journey.'

'Where will you go?'

'I will go...'

'Speak not,' interrupted Astur. 'Then your attendant can honestly say he does not know.'

Artakhshayarsha smiled. 'Now I know why my father chose you as Queen.'

Astur smirked. 'Your father chose me because I fell in the river.'

The young Prince stared at her. Astur shook her head. 'It is a long story.'

MEGABYZUS halted before the tall gates which were firmly barricaded.

'Well, Captain. It seems we are expected after all.'

'Then the messenger got here before us?'

'I do not see how, but I fear you are right.'

'Then we will attack the city?'

'Only as a last resort. Somehow, I suspect trickery. Whereas Artakhshayarsha will have known nothing of our approach, the messenger knows precisely how many men we have and must also know that they cannot hope to defend the city against us.'

'Then this is a trap?'

'Not a trap, Captain, unless they have requested help from Pasargades. Even then, it will be tomorrow before any reinforcements can get here. No, it will be something else.'

'But what?'

'I don't know. It just doesn't look right. I think somehow that we might be wasting our time attacking the city.'

'Could they have escaped?'

'There is but one road through the valley, Captain. They did not pass us coming in so that means, if they have fled, it will be north-east towards Pasargades.'

'Perhaps they mean to hide out there.'

'I do not think so. The coronation palace is poorly defended being far from Persia's borders.'

'Then further up the valley?'

'Unlikely. The valley rises to Kuh-i-Bul and will be impassable to the north at this time of year.'

'Then eastwards, across the mountains?'

'You jest, Captain. To the east is the Kavir; twenty-thousand square miles of dried-up salt marshes which have neither been crossed nor even charted. Even Artakhshayarsha is not that much of a fool.'

'Perhaps that is what we are meant to think.'

'Captain,' laughed Megabyzus. 'No-one ever returns from the Kavir. If the salt does not get you, the sun will. If you survive the sun, the sulphur pits will envelope you. Believe me, Captain, if Artakhshayarsha has gone into the Kavir then we might as well go home now.'

'Then he will be still in the city.'

'Almost certainly.' He stopped and stared thoughtfully at the distant peaks. 'However....'

THE valley narrowed as the couple climbed above Pasargades. Mountain eagles circled them, looking for a meal for the newborn egrets that would be sheltering somewhere high in the rocks above them. Already, the snow was visible in sheltered crevices. Snow which would soon vanish as spring progressed.

'You ride well,' observed Artakhshayarsha.

'My father taught me when I was a child, though I am well out of practice.' She held out her hand and, for the first time, the Prince saw the blisters.

'By Mithra, they look sore.'

'They are. But they will heal.'

'Not where we are headed. The salt and sulphur will get inside the skin and will destroy your hands.'

Astur shrugged. 'We have come too far to turn back now.'

'Are we wasting our time?'

'I hope not. Even if we are, it is better to die trying than to go dreaming of what might have been.'

'We must rest,' Artakhshayarsha announced.

'Not yet,' contradicted Astur. 'We must reach the head of the valley before nightfall. We will then have at least some warning of any approach.'

'But surely, no-one will follow us.'

'Don't be too sure. Megabyzus will not want to return to Artabanus and admit that he has failed to kill you.'

'Artabanus will not find out unless Megabyzus tells him.'

'You do not know Artabanus. He has spies in every camp. He will know and, if Megabyzus tries to deceive him, he will use it as an excuse to get rid of him. Listen well, Artakhshayarsha. If you value your life, never trust Artabanus.'

The Prince smiled. 'I will remember what you have said.'

'Come,' said Astur with a cheeky smile. 'I will race you to the top of the pass.'

MEGABYZUS stared at the city wall at Pasargardes. His Captain rode alongside. 'Do we attack, My Lord?'

'No, it is too quiet. Take a squad and search for tracks higher up the valley whilst I remain here. If Artakhshayarsha has fled, follow him and this time, do not fail me. Do not come back unless you have his head on your spear.'

The Captain wheeled his horse. 'It shall be as you have spoken, my Lord Megabyzus. At this time tomorrow, I will deposit his head at your feet.'

FOR two days and two nights, Astur and Artakhshayarsha headed northwards, hardly stopping for rest, eating only when they had to and drinking where they could. As they got onto lower ground, the temperature escalated and, by the time they reached the brown, sluggish Zdyandeh River, the heat was almost unbearable. Twenty miles to the north, they could see the hazy outline of the low range of peaks marking the edge of Persia proper. Beyond those hills lay only the Dasht-e-Kavir, the great sulphur lakes and salt marshes which reached almost as far as the Elburz hills at the southern end of the Sea of Caspia.

'We must stop and rest soon,' said Artakhshayarsha, rubbing his aching back and staring up at the scorching sun.

Astur looked back at the faint smudge of dust on the horizon. 'Not yet, my Lord King. I don't know who it is that Megabyzus has sent after us but they certainly know their job. Even our efforts at covering our tracks to mislead them at the river did not deceive them. It is as if they know exactly where we are headed.'

'Can we not cut across to Ecbatana from here? We could be there in a day or so.'

'We could. But we don't know who might be waiting for us. If the news has reached Artabanus that you have escaped Megabyzus, he will have alerted the city. We first need to give our pursuers the slip and then we will have time to make proper plans.'

'It's just this heat. I don't think I can go on much further.'

'You must. We cannot allow ourselves to get caught now.'

Artakhshayarsha glared at her. 'You are worse than my real mother ever was.'

'But a lot younger,' added Astur with a smile. 'Don't forget that I am only a year older than yourself. If I, a mere woman, can go on, then so can you.'

He sighed in resignation. 'How much further?'

She pulled a scruffy piece of paper out of her tunic. 'According to the rough map Artaynte drew for me, we should reach the mountains by tonight.'

'Then can we rest?'

'If you insist. However, there will be a full moon tonight and I recommend that we ride on through the night. If we can reach the southern edge of the Kavir by mid-morning, there is a chance we will lose them.'

'You go on,' he sighed. 'I've had enough.'

Astur nudged her mount close to him and grabbed him by the front of his gown. 'You are an Achaemenid King, Artakhshayarsha. Just remember that. Darius would not have given up so easily and neither would your father. If you have ever had any respect for either of them, you will stop this self-pity at once and do something useful for a change.'

He shrugged off her hand. 'I am old enough to decide. Stop treating me like a child.'

'Then stop acting like one and start pretending to be a King, or at least a man.' Digging in her heels, she cantered away from him.

Artakhshayarsha watched her go until she was almost a dot and then galloped after her. He would show her that he was no longer a boy but a man.

THE guide jumped from his horse and examined the marks on the ground. 'An hour ahead of us, Captain, and definitely just the two of them.'

'Good,' responded the officer. 'It will be dark soon and we shall surprise them by riding into the night and catch them as they sleep. I want the Prince. The rest of you may have the boy.'

The soldier grinned. 'What better incentive could we need?'

'Other than the gold that Megabyzus has promised? I suggest we just get the job done as quickly as we can and then return with their heads before he changes his mind.'

'As you say, Captain.'

'I will add a bonus,' the Captain smiled. 'A hundred gold darics to the man who brings me the head of Artakhshayarsha.'

ARTABANUS stormed around the palace at Shushan after hearing the latest news, his face dark with anger. 'Cannot anyone do as they are told these days?'

'But Megabyzus reckons he will bring their heads to you within the week,' reasoned his general.

'If he can catch them. It seems that young Artakhshayarsha has more brains than I gave him credit for.'

'With respect, Lord Artabanus. The men have found no trace of the Prime Minister either. I have tortured all the household but they will not speak.'

'Then torture them again. I will not be made a fool of.'

'But, sire, several of the men have already died from the beatings we have given them.'

'Have you started on the women?'

'Not yet, sire.'

'Then start immediately. Have them raped by the mercenaries in the public square.'

'And if they still remain stubborn?'

'Then do the same with their children. When a few have died, screaming, from their abuse, you should get the information we need.'

The general bowed. 'As you command, Lord Artabanus.'

'And bring in Harbona. I want to find out what the problem is with my proclamation.'

Within minutes, the King's faithful attendant was brought in.

'What have you done with my royal decree.'

Harbona bowed. 'Nothing, my Lord. I am unable.'

'Unable? What do you mean, unable? I issued a command that I be declared as King. What can be wrong with that?'

'With respect, my Lord, such a proclamation is not possible.'

Artabanus whirled round. 'Why not?'

'The King commanded it before he died,' clarified the attendant. 'It is written in the law that a committee of three agree all new proclamations of state. At least two must sign before it can be issued.'

'And who are these signatories?'

'The King, the Queen and the Prime Minister.'

Artabanus threw his arms in the air. 'But the King is dead. Darius killed him.'

'If you say so, my Lord Artabanus.'

'You doubt my word?'

'It is not for me to say.'

'You will sign the King's name.'

Harbona was horrified. 'I could not. To forge such a document would be outright sacrilege against Ahura-Mazda.'

Artabanus thrust the proclamation in front of him. 'Sign.'

Harbona held his head high. 'I will not unless so instructed by the Queen.'

'The Queen is dead.'

'Then Marduka must use the King's signet ring.'

'Marduka has run away after sharing in the murder of the King.'

'Marduka would not do that.'

Artabanus lost his temper completely and struck him across the face. 'You would dare to contradict my word?' He turned to the guards. 'Take this man outside and hang him.'

'What do we do now?' said the general after Harbona had been taken away.

Artabanus smashed his fist down onto the table. 'I will be King. I must find a way around Khshayarsha's law.'

'It will not be easy, my Lord. The other Princes will only accept you if your ascension has legal basis.'

'I know that, fool. Send out the search parties. Find Marduka and fetch him to me unharmed.' He smiled. 'Bring his woman along as well. Artaynte always was the King's best concubine. Perhaps if I begin to cut a few pieces off her pretty little body, Marduka will be eager to do all I ask of him.'

'An excellent idea, Lord Artabanus. We will find them at once.'

ARTAKHSHAYARSHA slipped from his mount as the sun rose on their right. Carefully, he tested his weight on the flat piece of ground before them and the whole area moved slightly. 'It's no good, we'll never find a way across.'

'We have to,' said Astur. 'We can't just keep going around the edge for evermore. Artaynte's map says that there is a track near here.'

He stood with his hands on his hips and surveyed the scene of desolation before them. 'Well, I can't see it. Are you sure this is the place?'

'Look for yourself. The track is just after the place where the river from the east drains into it.' She pointed. 'There is the river. The track must be here somewhere.'

Artakhshayarsha stared back at the plume of dust which relentlessly followed them. 'Then we had better find it soon. We don't have much time.'

Astur, from the back of Mercury, looked across the salt-wastes. At the edge, it was flat and looked solid. However, she knew that, under the thin surface crust of hardened salt, was a slimy, treacherous mud that would suck them under and either drown them slowly or trap them until the soldiers caught them and did as they wished with them. In the distance were islands of salt-encrusted rock which oozed yellow sulphur and gave off smoke and an acrid smell.

Artaynte had been very accurate in her description of this god-forsaken place. By legend, it was identical to the land of Sodom and Gomorrah after those cities had been destroyed by the fire and sulphur which had erupted from rift fissures and had fallen, as if from heaven, killing so many people. Astur shivered at the thought and nudged her horse along the edge of the stark, white desert. A small stream trickled from the hillside on her left and cleft the terrain with its erosive action before, somewhere out there, soaking into the desert floor and leaving a mineral deposit which would add to that already present.

Without thinking, she turned Mercury and rode into the deepening arroyo, the hooves splashing through the warm water. The stream bed was level and firm though the liquid was murky, stained by the mountain sands and clay. After a short distance, she turned and found that the entrance was no longer visible. Faintly, she could hear the voice of her step-son, calling to her.

'I'm here,' she shouted and her voice echoed around the walls of her unnatural-looking canyon. Trotting back, she met Artakhshayarsha who was almost frantic with searching for her. The cloud of dust seemed almost upon them as she caught his attention and beckoned. 'Follow me.'

Artakhshayarsha gripped her arm. 'We will be trapped.'

'There are many arroyos. They will not know which we have entered.'

'But if they see our tracks, they will follow us. We will not be able to escape.'

Astur looked him in the face. 'We have no choice.'

She rode off and, with a last look at the approaching riders who could now be seen clearly, less than a mile away, Artakhshayarsha rode after her.

THE Captain reigned to a halt at the edge of the Kavir. 'They must have gone in.'

'Then they are as good as dead. Should we follow them, just to make sure?'

'I think we should make an effort. We will split into pairs and search the canyons.'

The sergeant turned to the men. 'You heard the Captain. Spread out and search. Be back here by nightfall and we will camp over there beside the river and guard the exits. If nothing else, we can be certain they will not come out alive.'

THE full power of the sun blazed down upon Astur as she nudged her horse along the arroyo. The perspiration poured from her body as the blazing heat reflected from the white walls of the canyon and turned the narrow defile into a scorching furnace. She glanced up at the sky and knew that there were still many hours of day left and they would soon have to find shelter or collapse. Desperately, she fought the almost-overwhelming temptation to turn Mercury around and race for the entrance, now miles away, and burst out into the open where at least the slight breeze could cool her burning skin.

Inside the hood, her face felt as if it was blistering as the reflected heat blasted at her. Within her tunic and breeches, her skin was being chafed away by the coarse material already soaked on the inside with her intense perspiration. She stopped and looked at Artakhshayarsha who had given up the fight to resist and simply sat on his horse as it followed Astur's. He was the picture of abject misery.

'We must stop,' he muttered as his horse caught up with her. 'I am going to die.'

'You certainly will if we stop. We must keep going for a little longer. They may well still be following us.'

'I don't care anymore. I just want to lay down and wait for the end.'

Astur reached down and clutched at the reins of his horse. 'Not yet. You may be ready to die but I am not.'

The sudden movement was too much for Artakhshayarsha. With hardly a sound, he slipped from his horse and crashed to the ground, the hot, yellow water trickling close to his face.

Astur leapt from her own horse and knelt beside him. 'You must get up. We daren't stop here, they will find us.'

'I cannot,' he murmured softly. 'You go on. Leave me here to die.'

Carefully, with her small dagger, she cut a wide strip of material from the bottom of her long tunic and used a little of the precious water they had brought to moisten it and wipe it across his forehead. The rest of the liquid she dribbled between his parched lips. As she covered his head with the damp material to keep the sun off, she heard the sound of hooves. They seemed to echo around the canyon and she found it difficult to judge the distance that they were away. Leaving the Prince on the ground, she ran to his horse and pulled the long spear from the side of his saddle. Then, ignoring the hardened salt which was burning the exposed skin of her back, she forced herself into a narrow cleft in the salt mass where she could remain hidden until they were very near. Gradually, the hoofs came closer and closer until, with a cry, the men drew to a standstill some way away and stared at the prone form of Artakhshayarsha.

'Is he dead?' asked one of his companion as Astur trembled at what she was about to attempt.

'He looks it,' replied the other and nudged his horse forward at a trot. 'But where is the boy?'

'I am here,' Astur said and, holding the spear by the point, swung the heavy shaft with all her strength. The soldier's expression was a picture as he recognised Astur a second before the beam smashed him full in the face and pitched him from the saddle.

The other soldier hesitated and, before he could move, Astur ran towards him. He drew his sword and raised it into the air, ready to slash downwards at her. Astur reacted instinctively by screaming at the horse. Not expecting such an unusual development, the animal reared up and its rider's sword swung wide of the mark. Astur thrust upwards and the point of the spear entered his body just below the ribs. The downward movement of the horse forced the spear deep into his body and he fell sideways, dead before he crashed onto the ground. Astur turned on the balls of her feet, crouched like a wild cat, as the first man stumbled to his feet in a daze. His sword was in his hand as he stood over the prone Artakhshayarsha. She sprang at him before he could fully recover his senses and fell on top of him, her small knife in her hand. The man gasped as he hit the ground and Astur raised her arm to strike but it was not needed. She sat astride his chest and looked down at his still form, his neck at a strange angle.

Gradually, reaction set in and she shuddered and cried at what she had done. A hand touched her shoulder and she whirled round, her knife at the ready.

'Don't,' said Artakhshayarsha, falling backwards in his surprise. 'I just wanted to help.'

Her shoulders slumped. 'It's a bit late for that.'

Carefully, he helped her to her feet and held her close until she stopped shaking.

'Come,' he said eventually as he turned towards his horse. 'We must go further before the vultures arrive and attract unwanted attention.'

Astur shook her head. 'The vultures do not come here. Somehow, even the scavengers of the desert know which places to avoid.'

'We have two extra mounts,' remarked Artakhshayarsha. 'And water,' he said, shaking the dead mens' water bags.

'Collect their weapons,' said Astur suddenly. 'Put them on the spare horses. We may need them again.'

'Who needs an army?' smiled the Prince. 'When I have you?'

'I was angry,' said Astur sadly as she climbed back onto her horse.

He grinned. 'You must become angry more often.'

She lashed out with her tongue. 'I was not angry with them, you idiot, I was angry with you. Don't you ever fall down on me like that again.'

He bowed in mock submission. 'No, your Majesty.'

Astur suddenly saw the funny side of it and rode close to him.

'And, young man,' she added, pointing her index finger at him severely. 'If either of us ever comes out of this alive, don't you dare ever call me "mother".'

IMPOSSIBLE though it might first appear, the temperature continued to rise throughout the rest of that afternoon. The white sides of the arroyo seemed to collect the heat and then concentrate it within the confined space. In time, their sluggish stream crossed others and, gradually, they found themselves in a totally alien landscape where jagged sulphur and salt pillars were interspersed with bubbling pools of yellow brine.

'We can't go on,' complained Artakhshayarsha bitterly. 'We have no idea where we are or which way to go.'

'We must go on. I would rather like to hang on to my belly for a while longer and I'm sure you would like to keep your head.'

He looked over his shoulder at the empty salt waste. 'They can't still be following us, surely.'

'Don't underestimate Artabanus. He is greedy will do almost anything for power. Megabyzus is not quite as bad but he knows he dare not cross Artabanus at this stage. He will have issued very strict instructions to his men for them not to return without us.'

'And you think they know where we are?'

'They have done all along. They must have someone with them who is very good at tracking fugitives. They followed us across the mountains and the lower valley, didn't they?'

Artakhshayarsha nodded. 'You are right. But when do we stop?'

Astur looked up at the sun and sky and, standing up in the saddle, surveyed the scene around them. She pointed. 'When we reach those tall rocks.'

'Very well,' sighed the Prince and nudged his mount forward.

The rocks were, in fact, not rocks at all but a huge outcrop of salt and sulphur which looked as if it had been forced out of the bowels of the salt-lake itself. The surface was slimy and oozing a creamy substance and the horses shied away from it with obvious terror. Artakhshayarsha dismounted and strode over to the strange formation.

'It is hot,' he said, withdrawing his hand from it quickly. 'And it trembles a little.'

'Trembles?' queried Astur, staring at it.

'I think it is alive.'

Astur laughed. 'It cannot be. It is a rock.'

The laughter died in her throat as the vibration increased and steam and yellow smoke began to belch forth from fissures all around them. Artakhshayarsha staggered back, coughing and rubbing his eyes and then collapsed as Astur jumped from her mount and tried to help him to his feet.

'Go,' he said. 'It is the dragon at the centre of the earth. It is angry at our coming here.'

Astur had never experienced anything like it before, but the idea of a subterranean dragon did not seem logical to her as she struggled to drag her companion away from that trembling monstrosity. Instantly, everything went crazy. There was a loud explosion followed by a hiss as steam and yellow liquid burst into the air and Astur covered her ears and hardly noticed the horses as they bolted. The roaring and hissing seemed to go on forever as Astur leant over the Prince's prone form, trying to shield him from the blast and the debris which fell in small, sharp pieces around them. Now, she thought to herself, I know how Lot's wife must have felt while she was being turned into a pillar of salt.

The sky was dark around them as they were showered with semi-solidified globules of matter. Gradually, the noise and vibration increased until Astur thought she could bear it no more. Then, a sudden pain came to her back and she cried out in agony. She tried to find the source of the pain as it came again and again as lumps of hot sulphur burned her skin. Huddled over Artakhshayarsha's face she tried her best to protect him with her own body as the skin was being slowly stripped from her back and arms. There was no relief, nowhere to go nor hide, as her whole world became full of darkness, noise and pain. When she thought she could take no more, it abruptly stopped and she lay, panting, across the body of her King. Astur was barely conscious of the fact that the sky was clearing. She could not move as they were coated with a fine film of substance which was solidifying over them, the salt in it still burning her skin and flesh. Her eyes were searing and her throat choked as the sun was revealed again and she then knew that nothing could save them from a slow, agonising death.

THE horses trod carefully across the salt waste as the riders scanned the landscape for the two fugitives. Suddenly, one of the riders stared before touching his companions arm and pointing. His companion smiled, nodded and urged the horse forward. They had found what they were looking for.

ASTUR heard them coming. The sun had just risen again and she was surprised to discover that she was still alive after a night of constant torture. Beneath her, she could feel the gentle breathing of Artakhshayarsha and knew that he, too, had somehow survived the freezing hours of darkness.

She tried to open her eyes but found she could not, they seemed to be pasted together with the evil crust which had formed over them. It was the hoof-beats that she noticed first, drumming on the hard ground as they approached. As they got closer, she also heard voices in conversation and knew then that she would soon be dead, away from the dreadful pain which was racking her whole body. Surely, even having her belly ripped out could be no worse than this. In an last, desperate, bid to protect herself she peered through one narrow slit and was now certain that she was dying.

She had heard once that your whole life passes before your eyes at such a time. In her present dreams, she saw Marduka and Artaynte. She smiled inwardly. At least they would survive, wherever it was they were hiding. As the heat from the sun began to scorch down again, she blissfully passed into unconsciousness.

THE first rider stared at the lone horse which had remained while the others had flown.

'Is it the one?' asked Artaynte.

'It certainly looks like Mercury. Astur must be around here somewhere.'

The young Princess shielded her eyes from the sun and peered around her at the place where the sulphur geyser had recently erupted and covered everything in another layer of salt and sulphur hardening in the blistering sunlight.

'You look over there,' said Mordecai. 'I will try to catch the horse.'

Artaynte dismounted and felt the intense heat through the soles of her leather sandals as she searched around for any trace of her friend. Suddenly, she saw a piece of red cloth half-covered in the fallout.

'Mordecai,' she called. 'I have found her.' Frantically, she began to scrape away the deposit and check for life signs as her husband arrived and dropped from his horse.

'Water, Artaynte. Wash it off with cold water or you will damage her skin. It looks pretty raw to me.'

He dropped the two full water sacs beside her and Artaynte began to splash it onto Astur's back and arms.

'Artakhshayarsha is here, too,' she said.

'Are they alive?'

Artaynte nodded. 'Just. They will need shelter before the sun begins to blister the damaged skin.'

'There is no shelter here,' observed Mordecai as he scanned the landscape. 'We will have to get them clear of this place before we can do much to help them.'

'We cannot move them. They will die.'

'We must. I know not how long it will be before the geyser erupts again.'

By this time, Artaynte had them both free from their imprisoning crust and was gently smoothing cool water over Astur and Artakhshayarsha.

'It was the night that saved them,' remarked Mordecai. 'In this heat, they would have survived no more than a few hours. We must get them away from here.'

'Very well. I will wrap Astur in the water skin to keep her cooler. Artakhshayarsha does not seem too badly burned.'

'No. I think Astur prevented that by shielding him with her own body.' He looked around. 'Are you sure you can find your way out of here?'

Artaynte sighed. 'I must, for Astur's sake. And quickly.'

THE day became hotter as the three horses trotted slowly upstream along the arroyo that soaked up the water from the hills. Several times, Artaynte halted and went off to spy out the land. Once, they had to wait while horsemen rode nearby, still searching for the royal fugitive.

Artaynte was good. By high sun, they were out of the Kavir and riding for the low-lying hills to the west. By sunset, they were on the other side and they camped beside a stream into which Astur was laid to ease the obvious agony.

'Well?' asked Mordecai with concern.

Artaynte shook her head. 'It is a miracle they are alive at all, especially Astur. She must have been in terrible agony before she passed out.'

'And Artakhshayarsha?'

'I think he will live. It looks as if he was mainly overcome by the fumes. There seems to be little external damage.'

'Do what you can for Astur. She is still my little girl.'

Artaynte smiled. 'And my best friend. I will do everything

possible.'

IT took five days for the slow-moving group to return to Shushan. By the time they arrived, the Court had moved to Ecbatana for the summer. Artaynte went alone into the city. It was dark and eerie as she crept along by the palace wall but she eventually found a friend.

'Nehemiah,' she whispered. 'Are you alone?'

'Princess Artaynte,' he responded with surprise. 'They told me you were dead.'

She smirked. 'Not me, I don't kill that easily and neither does Astur.'

Nehemiah grabbed hold of her gown. 'Queen Astur? She is alive? Artabanus said you had all been executed for assassinating Prince Artakhshayarsha.'

'We didn't kill Artakhshayarsha nor anyone else for that matter.'

'Then who did?'

'No-one. Artakhshayarsha is also still alive.'

The young Jew sat down. 'Then...'

'Artabanus has a lot to answer for. It is he who murdered the King here in Shushan and arranged to have Darius put to death. Tell me, is Megabyzus back from Persepolis yet?'

'No, my Princess. Artabanus had asked him to stay there until the summer has ended so that he can be ready to leave for Egypt.'

'Have they rebelled again?'

Nehemiah nodded. 'It is Inaros of Lybia. He has taken control of the whole Nile Delta upon hearing of the death of the King. Artabanus had declared himself ruler of Egypt and Inaros wouldn't stand for that.'

'So, we have some time. I must find a way to get Astur and Artakhshayarsha into the city. Will you help me?'

'Of course. Bring them to the south gate an hour before dawn. The gatekeeper is a Jewish proselyte who sided with Marduka against Haman. He will let you in.'

'Very well. We will be there at the time appointed and will hide out in the Court of Women.'

THE weeks went by and, gradually, Astur and Artakhshayarsha got better. Soon, Astur was up and about, the last of her blisters now almost completely healed.

One day, Hathach rushed in to where she was bathing in cool water. 'Your Majesty, Artabanus has returned to Shushan.'

Astur's heart began to beat faster as she glanced towards Artakhshayarsha who lay on his couch being fed by Artaynte.

'How many are with us?' she asked quickly.

'About a dozen, your Majesty. You ordered us not to announce your presence until Artakhshayarsha was well enough to assume control himself.'

'Then we will remain silent. In another few days, the King will be fully recovered and in a position to challenge the authority of Artabanus.'

'It shall be as you have spoken, my Queen.'

ARTABANUS entered the city and spirits were high as there was usually a banquet upon the ruler's return to Shushan.

'Send messengers to Megabyzus,' he commanded as he strode into the palace. 'I want him to come to Shushan immediately. War has escalated in Egypt and I want them crushed.'

'As you command,' said the attendant, bowing.

'And start the banquet at once. I am weary from my journey.'

'Are the people to be invited, My Lord Artabanus?'

'Of course not. Khshayarsha treated the people of Shushan with too much kindness.' He paused as the servants rushed about to make preparations. 'And bring me all the girls from the harem. I have had a long and difficult journey and now feel in the mood for some sport.'

'There are but few, my Lord Artabanus. The King had the harem at Shushan reduced to just a handful to please the Queen.'

'King? Queen? I am King here now and there is no Queen unless I decide that one of the young ladies pleases me. Have them brought in to me immediately.'

Hathach bowed. 'As you command.'

He hurried from the room and down to the Court of Women as the food began to be served. As quickly as he could, he related the instructions of Artabanus.

'All the concubines?' queried Artaynte. 'He is becoming more of a dirty old man with each day that passes.'

'I must return immediately with the concubines else he will send guards here to find out why I am delaying.'

'Of course, Hathach,' replied Astur, deep in thought. 'However, I have no intention of letting anyone else suffer at his hands. Nehemiah, Mordecai, could you stay here in the Court of Women and look after the King?'

Both men nodded their agreement.

Astur called the others to her. 'Hathach, return at once to say that the concubines are on their way. Roxana, Elma, Keiri, Artaynte - listen carefully. We must keep him from coming here and finding the King, so this is what we are going to do.'

ARTABANUS of the Achaemenids looked up as the music started and then smiled with pleasure as the veiled concubines abruptly entered and began to parade seductively before him. One by one, they stopped before him, whirled around, and then continued to skip across the marble floor. Eventually, he heaved his bloated body onto one elbow and pointed. Roxana stopped and bowed before him. 'You wish for me to please you, my Lord?'

'Yes, my dear. Come closer.'

'Wouldn't you rather have me?' said a voice nearby and Artabanus turned to see the source.

'Princess Artaynte,' he managed to blurt out just before the melon hit him full in the face.

'What about me?' called Astur and Artabanus almost had a heart attack at the revelation that she was still alive.

'Get them!' he shouted and pandemonium broke out in the palace as Artabanus shouted for guards and all the girls threw things at them and then, just as suddenly as they had arrived, vanished from sight.

ASTUR and Artaynte slipped quietly through the gatehouse and up the stone steps as they heard the guards searching for them.

'Will the other girls get away all right?' asked the Princess.

'I think so. It is me they are really after. Did you see the look of shock on the face of Artabanus?'

Artaynte giggled. 'He looked as if he had seen a ghost.'

'I suppose he had, in a way. He was so sure he had killed me.'

'At least it might gain us time until Artakhshayarsha is fully recovered.'

'If we can keep away from them in the meantime.'

'I think so. Remember the mountain at Ecbatana. None of the men could keep up with us.'

'Yes, and we know all the secret ways of the palace and city walls having been in hiding for so long. Push through the passageway. Let us cross to the other side.'

Carefully and quietly, the two of them crept through the stone passage over the gateway and thence down the far side through the guards' quarters.

Astur peered out of the doorway before closing it again. 'There are a dozen or so of them standing outside Mordecai's old gatehouse. They think we are still in there.'

'I hope they don't know about the secret passageway.'

'I'm sure they don't. Give them time to go inside and we'll slip past them and into the city.'

One by one, the guards went into the gatehouse and then the two young women slipped into the shadows. Silently, they crept across the public square and along the narrow street leading to the market place. Halfway along it, a doorway was thrown open and they were caught. Torches flashed as they were dragged down stairs and then thrust into a large cellar before a group of men wielding swords and spears.

'Bring them to me,' shouted the one who was obviously the leader.

The two of them were roughly hauled across the floor and then thrust at the man's feet. Astur's heart beat frantically as she tried to work out who these people were.

'Now let us see who it is that we are about return to Artabanus on a skewer.'

One of the men snatched Astur's veil away and the leader's mouth dropped open.

'It is the Queen,' he gasped and stepped back in amazement

as others pushed near for a closer look.

'It cannot be,' said another. 'She is dead.'

'It is the Queen,' said Artaynte loudly. 'And she has returned to Shushan to save you all from Artabanus.'

'Princess Artaynte,' cried another at the sight of the second unveiled face. 'By Ahura-Mazda, we are saved.'

Astur smiled. 'Not yet, we are not. We must first save the King.'

'The King?' said a big man. 'The King is dead. I helped to bury his body.'

'King Khshayarsha is indeed dead. But we now have another King who will reward your loyalty well.' She paused to convince herself that she was doing the right thing. 'His son, Artakhshayarsha, is now King.'

'Artakhshayarsha is alive?'

Astur nodded. 'Alive and in the palace, though Artabanus is yet unaware of it. We must prevent him finding out until we are ready.'

The leader bowed before her. 'Your Majesty, we are at your command.'

'How many are you?'

'Upward of one thousand, your Majesty.'

'Not enough. Spread the word around the city tonight. Inform everyone that the King is alive. Tell them to gather before the palace at daybreak.'

'It shall be done, Queen Astur.'

FOR the rest of the night, the girls kept the guards tied up looking for them. Other women from the city joined in the game, too, and, soon, the palace was in total confusion.

Artabanus was furious. 'Don't tell me that you have not yet

found them yet.'

'We tried, My Lord. It would appear they are everywhere. It is as if they have the gods with them.'

'Superstitious nonsense. I have an army of thousands of men who have stood firm against Babylonians, Egyptians and Greeks alike. Now, it seems, they have a pair of females running rings around them. Are they men or mice?'

'They are tired after their long march from Ecbatana.'

'Then the sooner we catch those women the better for all of us. When I get my hands on them...'

'They can't keep running around forever, My Lord. They must have somewhere to return to.'

Artabanus suddenly stopped. 'By Mithra, you are right. Bring two men. I know just the place to find them.'

'But where, my Lord Artabanus. We have looked everywhere.'

'I fear, Captain, that there is one place you will have overlooked. Get your men. I will meet you in the Court of Women.'

AS the first light of dawn touched the Zagros, Astur and Artaynte crept into the palace unseen and passed into the Court of Women. Artakhshayarsha was now awake and being closely guarded by Nehemiah and Mordecai.

'Well?' asked the older man.

'I don't know, my father. The people of the city are with us. We just need a day or so until the King is back on his feet properly. Then, we can...'

Astur stopped as the door burst open and in the doorway stood Artabanus, spear in hand.

'So, now I have you all,' he said sadistically as he stepped towards them. 'I don't know how you managed to get away from us but now you are finished, all of you.'

With one glance round the room, he took in Astur, Artaynte, Artakhshayarsha on the bed, and the two men standing before it to protect him.

'Stand aside. I will become King this day.'

'No,' said Astur calmly. 'You will die this day.'

'Die?' He roared with laughter. 'It is not I who will die but you, my pretty one.' He turned towards her.

Astur defiantly faced him as he lowered his spear point until it almost touched her belly, the polished bronze tip glistening in the light from the oil lamps.

'Goodbye,' he said and thrust the spear forwards.

Unfortunately for Artabanus, Astur was no longer there. As he stabbed at her, she did a backwards flip and the spear slashed harmlessly in the air.

'Getting too old for this sort of thing, Artabanus?' she taunted from a few cubits away.

'Why, you,' he said as he lunged again.

Astur dropped to the floor and he missed yet again. He didn't see Artaynte move like lightning as she threw her body at the back of his legs and, before he could regain his balance, he was falling. Artabanus dropped into the water with a great splash and the two girls laughed as he fought to get to his feet. The laughter died away as their arms were gripped firmly from behind by guards.

Artabanus climbed from the pool and picked up his spear once more. 'Play games with me, would you? Treat me like a fool, eh? You men. Hold them to the pillars.'

Within seconds, both girls were firmly held from behind with their backs up against two of the tall columns, unable to move, as Artabanus gloated.

'Prepare to die, Astur, Queen of the Persians.'

'Artabanus. You are an animal.'

'I think you are probably right, my dear. However, now I must deal with you. I will kill you, of course, but not until you have watched your friend die.'

Artaynte swallowed as the point of the spear touched her. Her arms were firmly held, stretched out to the sides and she knew that she could do nothing at all to prevent herself being cut apart by this perverted egomaniac.

'Leave her,' begged Astur. 'I will do anything you ask.'

Artabanus pressed so that the point made a dent in Artaynte's skin, a slight pressure from sliding into her.

'You will sign over the Kingdom to me?'

Astur stared at her friend's skin that was about to be torn open. What had she said before? Never trust Artabanus. She had told everyone else this but was now contemplating a deal which she hoped would save her friend's life.

'Don't do it, Astur,' called Artaynte and the skin broke as she strained and then looked down at her own blood as it trickled down the blade.

'Torturing women again, Artabanus?' came the sudden voice from across the room and Astur stared in horror as Artaynte slid slowly down the pillar.

The old general turned and gaped. Artakhshayarsha swayed as he stood beside his bed and picked up a sword from the floor. Nehemiah and Mordecai, neither of them soldiers, stepped forwards but were pushed aside by the young Prince.

Artabanus smiled and held up his arm to the guards who had also stepped forward. 'I will take the boy.'

Confidently, Artabanus stepped towards the groggy Artakhshayarsha, his spear in his hand, Artaynte's blood still on the tip. Astur strained to break free but she was held firmly and had to watch as the two contestants faced each other. Help came from an entirely unexpected direction as Artaynte clutched one hand around her bleeding stomach and rolled across the marble floor towards Artabanus, catching him behind the legs as she had done before. Artabanus staggered and fell to his knees, and the young Prince struck out with all his might. Artabanus swayed slightly before pitching forward onto his face.

Without warning, Astur kicked out at her guard who grunted in pain and let go of her arm. Instinctively, she lashed out at the other guard who ducked and then raised his dagger.

'Stop!' shouted Artakhshayarsha as he swayed beside his couch pointing at the guard with his sword. 'Harm the Queen and I will have you dismembered alive.'

The man stared at Artakhshayarsha and then at the now-dead Artabanus before lowering his blade.

'Get the healer,' said Astur quickly to the guards. 'If Artaynte dies, you all die.' Astur dropped to her knees beside her friend and carefully turned her over. 'You, my girl, are going to have to practice that trick more often.'

'I'm sorry,' murmured Artaynte. 'I have failed you.'

'You did nothing of the sort. You saved our lives and, right now, you are going to take it easy while the rest of us take care of you.'

'Mordecai?'

The aged Jew dropped to his knees at her side. 'I am here.'

She groaned. 'I am dying.'

Astur pulled her friend's hands away and looked at the wound. It was neither deep nor wide but she had lost a lot of blood, mainly in her exertion to topple Artabanus.

'I fear you will live,' said the Queen as the healer entered and started to minister to Artaynte.

Astur walked over the where Artakhshayarsha sat on the couch, his head in his hands. She touched his shoulder gently and he looked up with tears in his eyes. Overnight, a boy had become a man, and a Prince had become a King.

'It is time,' she said eventually. 'We must go upstairs.'

He nodded. Together, they supported each other as the pair of them walked along the passageway and up the wide steps onto the balcony below which a crowd had already gathered. Astur stepped forward and leant on the low wall as a great hush came over the crowd.

'People of Shushan,' she called out as the last of the surprised murmuring died away. 'You have been through much these last few weeks. But I assure you that things will now be different. As you know, King Khshayarsha is dead and so is Prince Darius. I must also now tell you that Artabanus is also dead. Therefore...,' she hesitated because of the cheering. 'Therefore, I give you your new King.' Astur held out her hand as he stepped towards her. 'I give you King Artakhshayarsha of the Persians.'

The crowd cheered once more and Astur waited again until the noise died down before shouting; 'Long live King Artakhshayarsha of the Persians.'

'Long live King Artakhshayarsha of the Persians,' they repeated, over and over again as he leant on the balcony wall and tried to smile as the tears of joy ran down his face.

MEGABYZUS arrived five days later. He encircled the entire city with his troops and stood before the city gate. Scanning the walls, he saw the many archers who were ready to defend Shushan against attack. The city had no hope of withstanding a long siege and he knew it would soon fall. But, before a decision could be made, the gates opened a little and a solitary figure emerged and walked down the slope towards him.

'By the Lord Ahura-Mazda,' he said, shaking his head. 'I do not believe the evidence of my eyes.'

His aide nudged his horse forward. 'What is it, my Lord Megabyzus?'

'Look.' He pointed. 'It is the Queen.'

'The Queen? But my Lord, she is surely dead.'

Megabyzus smirked. 'Does that look like a ghost, Captain?'

'No, my Lord. It does not.'

'Then let us go and find out what the little witch is up to.'

He spurred his horse forward until he was within a few cubits of Astur and stopped, glaring down at her. 'How did you survive?'

Astur smiled. 'We Jews are not easy to destroy, Megabyzus. You should know that by now.'

'Why are you in Shushan?'

'To proclaim the new King.'

'New King?'

'Artakhshayarsha.'

Megabyzus looked up at the city in amazement. 'Artakhshayarsha is here?'

'Of course. He arrived with me.'

He looked puzzled. 'How do you mean?'

'He and I came from the Kavir.'

His eyes almost popped out of his head in surprise. 'You were with Artakhshayarsha in the Kavir? You were the one who led him from Persepolis and misled my troops for days?'

Astur grinned. 'It wasn't difficult. I told you before, you should train your men better, Megabyzus.'

She lifted the long spear she had carried from the city and the Captain dropped back a little and drew his sword for defence. Astur stuck the spear into the earth in front of Megabyzus's horse. 'This belonged to Artabanus.'

'Where is Artabanus?'

'Artabanus is dead. Artakhshayarsha has executed him for his treachery.'

'I see. And now Artakhshayarsha presumes to be King?'

'Of course. You and I do not have the required qualification, my friend. We are not of the Achaemenids so the other princes would not tolerate us for long.'

'And I suppose you just want us to go away again?'

She smiled up at him. 'Not at all. I want you to come to my banquet.'

The Prince stared at her. 'We will attack the city and destroy you all.'

'Advance past this spear and you will be shot down, Megabyzus. My orders to the archers on the wall are to aim only at you. Do you really want to be the first to die?'

For the first time, a look of uncertainty crossed the General's face as he looked up at the walls. 'What do you propose?'

'I propose a truce. If we fight, the great Empire will be divided and will not stand. Already, the Egyptians have rebelled and others will follow if they see the Persians lose power. You and I must fight side by side, not against each other.'

'And if I did submit to Artakhshayarsha, what is in it for me?'

Astur laughed aloud. 'You don't change, Megabyzus. Always the mercenary.'

'What is the deal?' he persevered.

'You become Satrap of Syria and the land beyond the River.'

'The land beyond the River? Damascus?'

She nodded. 'If it is your desire.'

Megabyzus thought long and hard. The Satrapy of Syria was the richest in the Empire. Whoever occupied Damascus, controlled the whole of the fertile crescent from Egypt to Babylon. It was, indeed, very tempting. 'And what of this rebellion in Egypt?'

'I will go to Egypt myself.'

He stared at her. 'You will go?'

'Naturally. I will appoint a Satrap there.'

'One who is strong enough to deal with Inaros?'

'No, I will appoint Inaros the Lybian himself. He has proved himself more than capable of taking the Nile Delta. He will now hold it for the Empire.'

'Will he do it?'

Her lips curled. 'I will find a way to...persuade him.'

'Astur,' he said quietly. 'You are some woman.'

'Then take my offer while it stands.'

For a moment, he thought about it and then slowly dismounted and stood before Astur. He drew his sword. Only two cubits separated them as he glanced up at the archers on the wall. The Queen had put her own life on the line to make peace. One quick slash and she was dead. But then, so was he. He stuck his sword into the ground beside the spear.

'Captain,' he shouted whilst still watching Astur. 'Have the men stand down. We are going to a banquet.'

THE crowds cheered as the procession wound its way into the city. Astur sat on Megabyzus' own white stallion whilst the general himself led it up the slope and in through the main gate. At the entrance to the palace, they were met by Mordecai and Artakhshayarsha who watched as Megabyzus helped down his Queen and presented her to the new King. For a while, the two men faced each other as the crowds held their breath until, with a smile, the King held out his arms. 'Welcome back to Shushan, my brother.'

Unity had once more come to Persia.

THE banquet was spectacular considering the shortness of the notice but Astur, as usual, had excelled and all were happy and satisfied; even Artaynte who was allowed to join them for a short time.

'Are you really going to Egypt?' asked Artakhshayarsha as they ate.

Astur nodded. 'With your permission, your Majesty. If Megabyzus goes, there will be a war which could last years, and Persia has better things to do with her resources.'

'But will it not be dangerous for you?'

'Probably,' Astur laughed. 'But after the events of the last few weeks, I think I can handle it.'

'I shall miss you.'

Astur suddenly turned and stared at the young man who had grown up almost overnight and who now ruled the Empire of his father. The previous bad feelings seemed all to have disappeared as she simply smiled in response.

'You will be back in time for my official coronation at Pasargades, won't you?'

'Sire, I would not miss it for the world.'

'I shall need a Queen,' he said suddenly.

'There are plenty to choose from among the princesses of Media and Persia. With respect to your mother, be careful you do not pick another Amestris.'

Artakhshayarsha laughed. 'I won't do that. In fact, I have already chosen my new Queen, if she will have me.'

'You have?' Astur looked surprised but happy. 'When?'

'Some few days ago.'

'Some...' she began to calculate. 'But...'

'Astur, Queen of the Persians, would you do me the honour of becoming my wife?'

'Me?'

'Why not? You are far better at this ruling business than I am.'

'But I regret I can give you no son.'

'It matters little. I will retain one concubine for that purpose, if you permit.'

Astur thought about it for a full minute. 'On one condition.'

The King looked wary. 'Which is?'

'That I get to choose her, and she is as ugly as a toad.'

King Artakhshayarsha laughed out loud. 'Astur, I do believe that you and I are going to get along fine.'

The Queen of the Persians smiled. 'You know something? That's what your father said.'

Epilogue

Artakhshayarsha, King of the Persians, ruled for fifty-one of his seventy years, the longest of all the Achaemenid Kings. This was partly because of his insistence at retaining peace wherever possible. During his long reign, Artakhshayarsha and Astur lived happily together in Shushan and the Empire prospered under their wise rule.

Contrary to everyone's expectations, in the fourth year of their reign the twenty-four-year-old Queen of the Persians gave birth to a son whom she insisted on naming Khshayarsha after her first husband and, two years later, another son - Darius.

At Astur's suggestion, Nehemiah was appointed to the post of chief attendant to Artakhshayarsha in the place of the murdered Harbona. Twenty years later, it was he who was to be responsible for the reconstruction of much of the Holy City, Jerusalem.

Sadly, the aged Mordecai never did return to the Promised Land as he had hoped but died only a year after Artakhshayarsha came to power and before Artaynte could produce a son for the hereditary position of Prime Minister. The beautiful Princess Artaynte, heartbroken at first, suddenly and mysteriously left Persia at the age of twenty and was never seen again by the Persians. She reputedly travelled to Europe, perhaps even England in search of precious tin, and what is thought to be her remains were unearthed during the 1950s in Central France where she had been buried with great honour and the dignity she so rightly deserved.

In the meantime, a treaty was drawn up between Persia and Greece whereby the Persians agreed to stay out of the Aegean and the Greeks promised to keep away from Asia. This treaty was repeatedly violated by the Greeks until, in the year 333 BC, the Macedonians under their leader, Alexander III, invaded Asia and raped and pillaged their way across the land. In the process, the Greeks deliberately desecrated or stole everything of any value and destroyed all the historical records of the previous generations. Unlike the conquering hero whom the Greeks portray in their poetry and sketchings, Alexander the Great (as they insisted upon calling him) was a squat, ugly, egomaniac of a man in the mould of Artabanus. He was almost permanently drunk and, at his premature death, he left behind so many illegitimate children all over the Empire that his succession was in doubt for many years.

When, specifically, Queen Astur died, no-one knows but somehow, a little of her spirit still remains in the Zagros Mountains and in the fertile valleys of Elam.

Other Books by the author:
    The Curse of King Arthur's Brood
    The Revenge of King Arthur's Brood
    The Return of King Arthur's Brood
    Plot
    Plot to War
    Plot for a King
    Requiem for a Princess
    Checkmate for Princess
    Aftermath of a Princess
    Escape Unto Death
    The Andromeda Burn
    The Andromeda Seed
    Return to Andromeda
    The Andromeda Trial
    Andromeda Time

Made in the USA
San Bernardino, CA
23 April 2019